BEATING THE
LUNCH BOX
BLUES

BEATING THE
LUNCH BOX
BLUES

J. M. HIRSCH

FOREWORD BY RACHAEL RAY

RACHAEL RAY BOOKS

ATRIA

NEW YORK   LONDON   TORONTO   SYDNEY   NEW DELHI

ATRIA PAPERBACK

A Division of Simon & Schuster, Inc.
1230 Avenue of the Americas
New York, NY 10020

First Rachael Ray Books / Atria Paperback edition September 2013

RACHAEL RAY BOOKS / ATRIA PAPERBACK and colophon are trademarks of Simon & Schuster, Inc.

For information about special discounts for bulk purchases, please contact Simon & Schuster Special Sales at 1-866-506-1949 or business@simonandschuster.com.

The Simon & Schuster Speakers Bureau can bring authors to your live event. For more information or to book an event contact the Simon & Schuster Speakers Bureau at 1-866-248-3049 or visit our website at www.simonspeakers.com.

Designed by Jane Archer
Food photography by Matthew Mead

PRINTED IN THE USA

10 9 8 7 6 5 4 3 2

Library of Congress Cataloging-in-Publication Data is available.

ISBN 978-1-4767-2672-4
ISBN 978-1-4767-2673-1 (ebook)

*To Parker, whose awesome appetite
for fun and food started it all.*

Contents

FOREWORD BY RACHAEL RAY

Looking for a way to cure your lunch box blues? You're not alone. J. M. Hirsch understands the frustration we all feel when scrambling for delicious yet healthy options for lunch. *Beating the Lunch Box Blues* is the perfect solution to this dilemma. Flip through these pages full of creative and easy lunch ideas and you'll see that the second meal of the day doesn't have to be conventional, monotonous, or time-consuming. J. M. Hirsch is an innovative thinker who knows how to spice up any lunch in no time and he's had years of experience as the food editor for The Associated Press and as the father of a finicky eater! So if you think you'd love to bite into a Shrimp Quesadilla, a Barbecue Chicken Sandwich, or a Pesto Grilled Cheese at noontime, you've come to the right place.

INTRODUCTION

Nobody wants a lunch cookbook. Especially not a lunch box cookbook. Because in the morning rush, not even the most obsessive compulsive among us is going to break out a recipe to bang out a brown bag special. Busy people need ideas. And lots of them. If they're healthy, fun, easy, and fall on the hipper end of the foodie spectrum, even better. And if they're fun enough for the kids, but delicious enough for adults? Bonus! That's what *Beating the Lunch Box Blues* is—an idea book to inspire anyone daunted by the daily ordeal of packing lunch, whether for yourself or your kids. Now, if you're one of those people who somehow finds the time to craft sandwiches into cutesy animals, or carve cheese into flowers and hearts . . . Congratulations! And good luck with your therapy. Now go away.

Seriously?

I'm a working parent who can't dedicate quite that much energy to my 9-year-old's lunch. Or my own. I'm pretty sure that doesn't make me a bad dad. But I also refuse to cede control to the packaged and processed lunch "kits" of the world. Or even to the monotony of a day-after-day-after-day PB&J. And for the record, at the start of a crazy day, being a food editor and cookbook author doesn't buy me any extra time or energy for lunch duty.

My search for a middle ground is what prompted me to start my blog, Lunch BoxBlues.com, a daily chronicle of my son's lunches. It seemed kind of silly at first. But as I got increasingly creative about what I packed for him, readers responded. Duh! Turns out I wasn't the only person sometimes overwhelmed by the challenge of assembling great lunches.

And that was the seed for this un-cookbook, a collection of hundreds of delicious ideas for thinking outside the (lunch) box. Since most people pack lunches in the morning, and mornings tend to be pretty crazy, I kept the format super user friendly: photos with tips and ideas, not recipes. Because you don't need a recipe to know that a grilled cheese with Manchego and fig jam with a side of fruit salad splashed with balsamic is a delicious lunch. Or that kids and adults alike will go nuts for a DIY taco kit made from leftover chicken or steak, whole-wheat tortillas, shredded cheese, sour cream, and veggies. The result is a cookbook-meets-flipbook approach to thinking about lunch, allowing you to page through fresh, healthy ideas for awesome, affordable meals.

I also slipped in 30 recipes for fast and flavorful dinners. Because great lunches often are built from the leftovers of killer suppers. A dinner of roasted pork tenderloin gets a day-after transformation into a pulled pork sandwich with just a couple forks and a bottle of barbecue sauce. Leftover sloppy Joes? Mix in canned beans for a thermos-ready chili that can be accompanied by tortilla chips and tomato wedges. And for convenience, each dinner recipe is paired with lunch ideas that use its leftovers.

When packing lunches overwhelms you, it helps to remember that it's just another meal. In other words, anything goes. Get beyond old-school notions of what a lunch is supposed to be, and you'll have tons of options. And even the most creative of those choices doesn't have to be difficult or time consuming. I never spend more than 5 or 10 minutes packing lunch.

What we feed ourselves and our children matters. Quality, healthy food doesn't just fuel busy brains, it also broadens our understanding of the world. Five or 10 minutes may not seem like much, but that's all it takes to assemble a good—and good for you—lunch. And I consider it time very well spent.

the tips

Having logged several years in the lunch box trenches, I've learned a few tricks for keeping myself sane. Most of the time.

MAKE TOO MUCH DINNER

In other words, cook once, eat twice. Or more. Leftovers make packing lunch so much easier, it just makes sense to build them into your dinner plans. After all, boiling up extra pasta on spaghetti night or roasting a larger chicken doesn't require any extra effort. This is true when making breakfast, too. Extra pancakes and waffles make great "bread" for sandwiches.

TRUST CRAZY IDEAS

Try to trust—or at least sometimes indulge—the occasional crazy idea. My son dreamed up the idea of a pretzel sandwich, so I gave him peanut butter and whole-grain pretzels on whole-wheat bread. He loved it. He loved that I'd listened to him. He didn't care that I'd made it healthy.

COMPARTMENTALIZE

Lunch boxes once were just that—boxes. Today, most are modeled at least in part after Japanese bento boxes, which have multiple containers and compartments. Search these out, because kids (and adults) love this approach to packed lunches. Having choices makes lunch more interesting. It also spurs creativity when you're packing them.

DON'T BE AFRAID OF THE COLD

If you have a thermos, great. If you don't, no big deal. Plenty of the meals you usually eat hot also taste great cold. My son loves cold leftover pasta carbonara. I think of it as an Italian version of cold Asian peanut noodles.

BREAK IT UP

Warm lunches can be tricky to pack. Popping them in a thermos may seem like a good idea, but many can't handle the heat without getting soggy. The solution? Break up the components. Pack hot sandwich fillings that are moist—such as barbecue pulled pork—in a thermos with the bread on the side. At lunch, just assemble and enjoy.

INVOLVE THE EATER

When practical, the person eating the lunches should be involved in the food shopping, prepping, and packing. The sense of ownership this fosters pays dividends when it comes to getting them to actually eat the food. Shopping and cooking with kids isn't always fun and easy, but what about raising children is always fun and easy?

Packing lunch for children? Here are some kid-specific tips.

PICK YOUR BATTLES

When your children say they don't like something you packed for them, trust them and thank them for trying it. Save the green bean battles for dinner, when you (and not their snotty-nosed friends) are there to model good eating habits.

THINK DIY

Kids love assembling their own meals. That's why packaged lunch "kits" are so popular. But it's cheaper and healthier to create your own DIY lunch kits. A selection of crackers, cheeses, hummus, peanut butter, jam, and deli meats can become a mix-and-match cracker stack lunch. Or whole-wheat tortillas with sliced leftover steak, cheese, sour cream, and guacamole can be a build-a-taco kit. And the DIY approach is fun for adults, too.

SKIP THE KID FOOD

It doesn't exist. Or rather, it shouldn't. "Kid food" is nothing more than a marketing ploy to try to get you and your kids hooked on a food company's over-processed, overpackaged, and overpriced products. Give kids real food with real flavor. They'll eat it, especially if you do, too.

IGNORE THE PRESSURE

Don't get sucked into "But Hulga Mae gets to bring cotton candy and Big Macs for lunch every day!" fights. I try not to demonize the other kids (or their awful lunches) with a simple, "Every family makes different choices." It may not lessen your kid's desire for his classmate's lunch, but it's the truth.

the gear

Selecting lunch gear used to be simple. Stuff your lunch into a paper bag and call it a day. If kids were part of the equation, grab the box decorated with whichever movie, television, or toy character the little ones were most smitten with. Done.

Things are a bit more complicated today. Lunch box styles vary from soft-sided cooler bags to Japanese-inspired bento boxes, even Indian tiffin canisters. They can have built-in ice packs. They can be microwave-safe. They can be made from recycled bisphenol-A-free, lead-free, phthalate-free, PVC-free plastic. They can be forged from 18-gauge stainless steel. Some adult versions even come with their own cheese boards and wineglasses.

So how do you choose? Much depends on the types of foods you pack and how you pack them, as well as when and where you eat them. But there are some general tips that can help you sort it all out regardless.

DISHWASHERS RULE

If it isn't dishwasher safe, don't buy it. Even if you don't use the dishwasher, this tells you something about the quality and durability of a lunch box item.

MULTIPLES MATTER

Get more than one of everything. This makes life much easier on those days when you forget or just don't have time to wash the gear used the day before.

LUNCH BOXES

Soft-sided insulated cooler bags are the way to go. They are affordable and come in all shapes and sizes. They also are durable and easy to clean. Look for one with two compartments. This makes it easier to segregate items such as easily bruised fruit, or a thermos of warm soup and a cold yogurt cup.

FOOD CONTAINERS

These are the jars, boxes, and other containers the food goes in. Be sure to get a variety of shapes and sizes to accommodate different foods. And at least some should be watertight for packing sauces, dips, puddings, and other liquids.

For a budget option, go with plastic food storage containers, which are cheaper to replace if lost. If you don't care for plastic, there also are plenty of stainless-steel options. These tend to be pricier, but are indestructible, kid-friendly, and dishwasher safe. My favorite is the LunchBots brand, available in every conceivable size and shape.

Plenty of companies also sell lunch "systems" or sets of small containers that fit together and pack easily in an insulated bag. These sets offer less versatility than when you assemble your own collection of containers, but they work great. Laptop Lunches makes a wonderful food-safe plastic bento kit.

DRINK BOTTLES

Even if all you ever pack is water, an insulated drink bottle is a good idea. Insulated bottles don't sweat. They also give you the flexibility to pack warm or cold drinks, such as hot cocoa or smoothies.

THERMOSES

It's best to have two—a conventional narrow thermos for soups and other easily spilled items, and a wide-mouthed jar for larger foods such as warm sandwich fillings or meatballs.

When selecting a thermos, be sure to check its thermal rating, which indicates how long it will keep items hot or cold. This is important information you'll need for keeping the food you pack safe to eat.

Perishable cold foods must be kept below 40°F. Hot foods should be held at above 140°F. Once the temperatures go outside these ranges, the food is safe for another two hours.

To use this information, figure out what time of day the lunches you pack will be eaten. Count back to the time of day the lunches are packed. This is how long you need to keep the food hot or cold.

One final tip about thermoses. They hold their temperatures best if you prime them before adding food. Packing soup or another hot item? Fill the thermos with boiling water for a few minutes to heat it up, then dump out the water and add the food. Filling it with yogurt or something that needs to stay cold? Place the empty thermos in the freezer for a few minutes first.

UTENSILS

This is not the time to break out the good silverware. But I'm also not a fan of disposable plastic, which breaks easily and has a lousy eco footprint. Instead, grab some inexpensive stainless-steel utensils at the bargain or secondhand shop.

ICE PACKS

Even if you're using an insulated lunch bag, an ice pack is a good idea, especially when packing lunches when it's hot out. As with everything else, get several so you always have one ready to go. I prefer rigid packs, rather than soft. The soft ones puncture more easily and can freeze in odd, hard-to-pack shapes.

the book

If a book requires a user's manual, the writer has failed. So while I won't tell you how to use this book, I will share what I was thinking as I cobbled it together.

THE LUNCHES: There are 162 of them. Though most of the lunches are built on a theme, they aren't intended as menus. Flip through, get inspired, make them your own, pack what works, eat what appeals.

THE DINNERS: There are 30 of them. By design, they make a lot of food. The idea is not to feed a crowd, but to feed a family of four plus provide ample leftovers, the building blocks of great lunches. Don't need that much? The recipes are easily halved. Each dinner is followed by lunch ideas inspired by its leftovers. Don't feel like making my recipe? You don't need to. The lunch ideas work with any similar leftovers.

THE MICROWAVE: Adults who brown bag it often have access to a microwave to reheat their lunches. This makes packing lunch easier. But I didn't want to exclude kids, who almost never have this option. So the ideas in this book generally assume the food will be eaten cold or be heated at home and kept warm in a thermos.

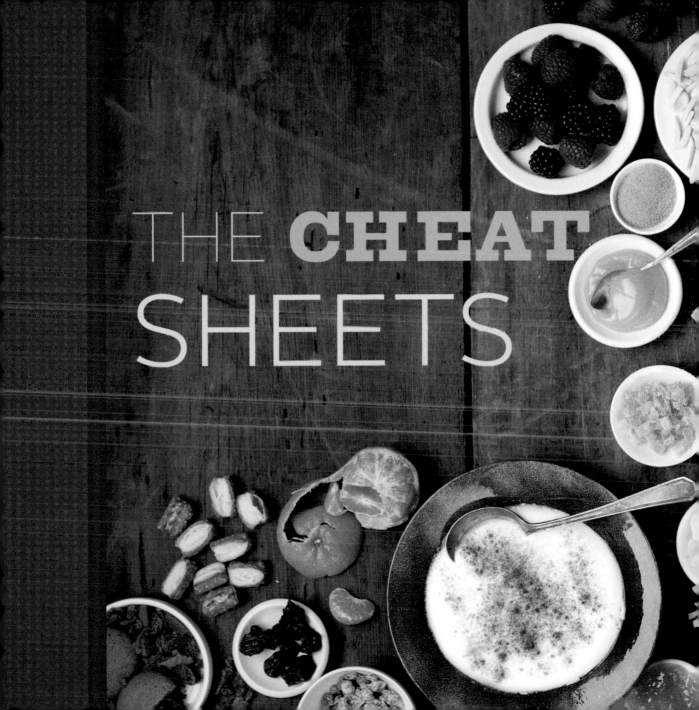

THE CHEAT
SHEETS

feel-good convenience

When we're trying to get through yet another hectic morning, convenience foods can be an important part of what keeps us sane, especially when they are convenience foods you can feel good about.

1. POPCORN—Even when dusted with "cheese" and salt, popcorn is still a fun whole grain.

2. NORI CHIPS—Seaweed (the same type used in sushi), seasoned and cut into chip-like strips. Salty, crunchy, addictive, and fewer than 20 calories per pack.

3. ROTISSERIE CHICKEN—Grab one a week to use just for lunches.

4. RICE CAKES—Prepare for an '80s flashback. Except this time they taste good and are whole grain.

5. SALSA PACKETS—Ketchup may not make the cut as a vegetable, but salsa does. Add a few baked corn tortilla chips and you get whole grains and veggies.

6. JERKY—Low in fat, calories, and sugar, but high in leave-them-feeling-full protein. You can even get organic,

turkey, vegan, salmon, and alligator(!) varieties.

7. DELI MEATS—Say what you will about them, but most varieties of ham, turkey, and chicken are low in fat and calories. And they are infinitely versatile. Look for varieties made without antibiotics or added nitrates and nitrites.

8. FRUIT POUCHES—Pureed fruit that you suck from an opening at the top. Some varieties even include veggies.

9. BARS—These require research. Many bars, especially granola, are loaded with fat, sugar, and processed junk. Look for bars with unprocessed fruits, nuts, and seeds, little or no sweeteners, and that have under 200 calories.

10. PHYLLO PASTRY CUPS—Low-cal, versatile, and fun. Fill them with egg, meat, and cheese for quiche, or peanut butter and jelly for PB&J poppers.

leftover by design

Easy, delicious lunch packing relies on leftovers. Which is why there are certain dinner foods I always make sure to cook too much of.

1. CHICKEN—Extra breasts and thighs equal easy wraps, salads, sandwiches, and soups.

2. STEAK—Cook the extra only to rare so it won't get tough when reheated for tacos and grilled cheese in the morning.

3. PASTA—Shape is irrelevant. Kitchen shears turn long strands into easy bites for small mouths.

4. RICE—It can be salad or stir-fry or even a patty. While you're at it, keep packs of heat-and-eat brown rice on hand.

5. COUSCOUS—It takes just 5 minutes to make, but has infinite uses. And for salads, cold leftover couscous is even better than freshly made.

6. GRILLED OR ROASTED VEGETABLES—Have them hot for dinner, then cold in a salad or wrap for lunch.

mix it up

Yogurts with granola or fruit "mix ins" are pricey and usually loaded with sugar.

Here are 25 easy ideas for yogurt toppings.

And if you pack a few toppings, you've got a DIY yogurt parfait.

1. Granola
2. Healthy breakfast cereal
3. Dried cranberries
4. Dried cherries
5. Mini pretzels
6. Chopped dates
7. Slivered almonds
8. Unsweetened jams
9. Applesauce
10. Fresh berries
11. Chopped dried apricots
12. Flaked coconut
13. Banana chips
14. Sunflower seeds
15. Cocoa powder
16. Graham crackers
17. Lemon curd
18. Chopped candied ginger
19. Mandarin orange segments
20. Crushed gingersnap cookies
21. Cinnamon
   (and a pinch of sugar)
22. Whole-berry cranberry sauce
23. Leftover cinnamon-sugar toast
   (cubed)
24. Mango chutney
25. Crumbled mini rice cakes

too cute to eat?

For adults, mini foods make for easy portion control and convenient packing. For kids, it's all about the novelty; they love little things. Whatever your motivation, start by checking out the produce section, which is jammed with "baby" fruits and vegetables. Even bread and cheese can be shrunk.

1. Baby cucumbers
2. Baby bell peppers
3. Cocktail bread (for cheese and "crackers" or mini PB&J)
4. Baby bananas
5. Bocconcini and other small varieties of mozzarella
6. Mini bagels
7. Cherry and grape tomatoes (duh!)
8. Baby carrots (double duh!)

the greatest thing since sliced bread

Sometimes all it takes to transform the same old sandwich is breaking free of your sliced loaf rut. Consider these alternatives next time you make a sandwich.

1. WAFFLES—Keep a box of frozen on hand, then toast or grill them (think grilled cheese).

2. PANCAKES—Make extra at breakfast, then smear them with PB&J.

3. CORN TORTILLAS

4. FLOUR TORTILLAS

5. FRENCH TOAST—Same as with pancakes; make extra. Particularly good with ham and cheese.

6. BISCUITS

7. DINNER ROLLS

8. NAAN

in a jam?

Need to mix it up a bit with the day-in-day-out PB&J? Wander the jam aisle and discover a world beyond strawberry jam and grape jelly.

Then head over to the international aisle. Nothing same old about the sandwiches you'll make with the jams found here.

And after you've paired them with various nut butters, try any of them on a grilled cheese.

1. Pineapple, banana, and passion fruit spread
2. Fig preserves
3. Apple butter
4. Apricot raspberry preserves
5. Creamed honey
6. Guava jelly
7. Mango jam
8. Muscat grape jelly

feeling nutty?

The peanut's monopoly on the nut butter world is broken. These days, there are tons of spreads for smearing on your bread. Some are even suitable for lunches where nuts are a no-go zone. But be sure to read labels and check school regulations first.

1. **ALMOND**
   (closest in taste to peanut)
2. **CASHEW**
   (so rich and creamy it will blow your mind)
3. **SUNFLOWER SEED**
4. **SOY NUT**
5. **SESAME SEED**
   (often called tahini)
6. **PISTACHIO**
7. **HAZELNUT-CHOCOLATE**
   (for when you're feeling indulgent)
8. **WALNUT**
9. **MACADAMIA**
10. **MARCONA ALMOND**

FEELING
FOWL

SWEET-AND-SOUR
CHICKEN

Takeout is easier, but not tastier. Nor as good for you (red food coloring, anyone?). Plus, I've streamlined the recipe to make your work as sweet as the sauce. Not in the mood for rice? This is delicious over egg noodles, too.

½ cup **all-purpose flour**

1 teaspoon **ground ginger**

1 teaspoon **garlic powder**

Kosher salt and **ground black pepper**

3 pounds boneless, skinless **chicken thighs**, cut into 1-inch chunks

3 tablespoons **canola or vegetable oil**

1 large **yellow onion**, thinly sliced

16-ounce bag frozen mixed **bell pepper strips**

2 cups shredded **carrots**

20-ounce can **pineapple chunks in unsweetened juice**

½ cup packed **brown sugar**

½ cup **red wine vinegar**

2 tablespoons **cornstarch**

Cooked rice, for serving

In a large bowl, mix together the flour, ginger, garlic powder, and 1 teaspoon each of salt and pepper.

Add the chicken, then toss until lightly but completely coated. It should use all of the flour mixture.

In a large sauté pan over medium-high, heat the oil until it shimmers. Cover a wire rack with paper towels.

Working in two batches to avoid crowding the pan, add the chicken and fry for 4 minutes per side. Transfer to the rack and repeat with remaining chicken.

When all of the chicken is browned, increase the heat to high and add the onion, peppers, and carrots. Sauté for 10 minutes.

In a small bowl, whisk together the juice from the pineapple, the brown sugar, vinegar, and cornstarch. Add to the pan and stir until thick, about 1 minute.

Add the chicken and pineapple chunks. Simmer for 2 minutes. Serve the chicken and sauce over rice.

Don't forget the bread and butter.

Blend leftover sweet-and-sour chicken, veggies and all, with mayo for a tangy chicken salad.

Find wasabi peas and Asian cracker blends in the grocer's international aisle.

ONE DINNER
TWO LUNCHES

Keep the Asian theme going with a seaweed salad. Grocers sell it fresh alongside the sushi. Shelf-stable versions are found with the natural or international foods.

Just add chicken broth and a splash of hot sauce to turn leftover sweet-and-sour chicken (even takeout) into hot-and-sour soup.

A grapefruit spoon is all you need to eat kiwis mess-free.

SWEET-AND-SOUR CHICKEN SALAD

HOT-AND-SOUR SOUP

THAI CURRY BARBECUE CHICKEN THIGHS

Start to finish: **20 MINUTES**
(PLUS OPTIONAL MARINATING)

Servings: **4 MAINS, PLUS LEFTOVERS**

The simple barbecue sauce used in this recipe blends the flavors of peanut satay and traditional barbecue. I like it on chicken thighs, but it's delicious on any cut.

Don't do peanuts? Any nut butter or alternative can be substituted, including soy nut butter or even tahini (made from sesame seeds).

Because the sauce packs tons of flavor and is low acid, the chicken can be flavored with it immediately before cooking or can marinate in it all day.

This recipe calls for broiling, but the chicken also can be grilled. Aim for 7 to 8 minutes per side over medium-high heat. And be sure to oil the grill grates especially well.

4-ounce jar (just shy of ½ cup) Thai red curry paste

Juice of 1 lime

¼ cup smooth peanut butter

¼ cup water

1 teaspoon kosher salt

¼ teaspoon ground black pepper

3 pounds boneless, skinless chicken thighs

In a large bowl, mix together the curry paste, lime juice, peanut butter, water, salt, and pepper. Mix until a smooth, thick paste forms.

Add the chicken thighs to the bowl, being sure to unfold them. Use your hands to rub the sauce onto the meat, covering it entirely.

The meat can be cooked immediately, or marinated for up to a day.

When ready to cook, heat the oven to broil. Line a rimmed baking sheet with foil, then set a wire rack over it. Coat the rack with cooking spray.

Arrange the chicken on the rack. Broil on the oven's middle rack for 6 minutes, then use tongs to flip the chicken. Broil for another 6 minutes.

Shredded carrots, raisins, and slivered almonds tossed with vinaigrette make an easy barbecue-friendly salad. Use a creamy dressing to turn it into a slaw.

Fresh strawberries are fine. Splashed with balsamic vinegar they are fantastic. Add fresh mint and you've got an OMG side.

Apple slices can be smeared with any nut butter for an easy, filling snack. Add a sprinkle of cinnamon-sugar to make them a dessert.

You'll feel good (or at least better) about chips when they are made from veggies.

ONE DINNER
TWO LUNCHES

Thinly sliced red onion and a hefty smear of hummus are the perfect complements to leftover barbecue chicken.

Heat-and-eat brown rice, canned beans, and chopped barbecue chicken? Heaven! Need moisture? Add bottled BBQ sauce.

BARBECUE CHICKEN SANDWICH

BBQ CHICKEN AND RICE

CHICKEN CAESAR SALAD WRAP

The best Caesar dressings don't come from bottles. But busy mornings aren't the time to bust out the anchovies to make it fresh, so find a brand you like and go with it.

A bit of nut butter transforms empty-calorie cookies into a filling, high-protein snack you don't have to feel quite as guilty about.

Salads don't get much simpler than chicken Caesar. Chicken + chopped romaine + dressing. Just wrap and eat!

FRIED TOFU POCKETS WITH CHICKEN

Edamame ain't just for restaurants, either. Buy them in the freezer section. Nuke them, pop them in a thermos with some salt, and enjoy. Many restaurants also serve edamame cold. If that's your style, you can skip the thermos step.

You've seen them at the sushi bar, now see them in your lunch box. Fried tofu pockets are like Asian pita pockets, but made from protein instead of carbs.

Buy them at the Asian market—or a sushi bar—then stuff as you see fit (anything goes) and serve them cold. My filling? Heat-and-eat brown rice tossed with chunks of chicken, rice vinegar, and sweet-and-sour sauce. Easy and delicious.

TURKEY
SLOPPY JOES

Start to finish: **30 MINUTES**

Servings: **4 MAINS, PLUS LEFTOVERS**

Prefer the big taste of beef in your Joes? Substitute lean ground beef. Or bison. Or a blend. Sloppy Joes are a total what-have-you recipe. Somebody in the family off carbs or gluten? These are awesome in lettuce wraps, too.

Don't be intimidated by the number of ingredients. This recipe comes together effortlessly in minutes.

12-ounce jar roasted red peppers, drained

1 cup tomato sauce

8 ounces white button mushrooms

1 small yellow onion

¼ cup ketchup

2 tablespoons Worcestershire sauce

1 tablespoon brown sugar

6 anchovy fillets

4 cloves garlic

1 teaspoon mustard powder

1 teaspoon hot sauce

1 tablespoon olive oil

3 pounds ground turkey

Kosher salt and ground black pepper

4 burger buns

Shredded cheddar cheese

In a blender, combine the red peppers, tomato sauce, mushrooms, onion, ketchup, Worcestershire sauce, brown sugar, anchovies, garlic, mustard powder, and hot sauce. Puree until smooth, then set aside.

In a large sauté pan over medium-high, heat the oil. Add the ground turkey and brown, breaking up any chunks, for 10 minutes.

Add the tomato–red pepper mixture, stir well, then bring to a simmer. Cook for 5 minutes, then season with salt and pepper.

Spoon the sloppy Joes onto the buns and top with cheese.

Sloppy Joes are like stew—they taste even better the next day. And just add beef or chicken broth to turn them into a substantial stew.

Just add canned beans and sloppy Joes become chili.

ONE
DINNER
TWO
LUNCHES

Wimpy salads need not apply for this lunch. Sliced tomato and fresh mozzarella are the way to go.

A robust take on a simple green salad: chopped fennel and avocado, tossed with vinaigrette and black pepper.

IODIZED SALT

IODIZED SALT

ZED

NEXT-DAY SLOPPY JOES

SLOPPY JOES CHILI

CHICKEN PICCATA
WITH **RED PEPPER–CAPER SAUCE**

Start to finish: **40 MINUTES**

Servings: **4 MAINS, PLUS LEFTOVERS**

Fast, easy, wonderfully flavorful, and endlessly versatile. Feel free to substitute mushrooms for the red peppers if that's more your style.

Store leftover chicken separate from the sauce; that way the chicken can be used for any number of lunch ideas, including sandwiches.

4 boneless, skinless chicken breasts

Kosher salt and **ground black pepper**

1 cup **all-purpose flour**

1 teaspoon **garlic powder**

4 tablespoons **butter**

2 **red bell peppers, cored and thinly sliced**

1 medium **yellow onion, thinly sliced**

3 cloves **garlic, minced**

1 tablespoon chopped fresh **thyme**

3 tablespoons drained **capers**

½ cup **white wine**

Heat the oven to 400°F. Line a rimmed baking sheet with foil.

Carefully slice each chicken breast in half horizontally to create 2 thin halves, for a total of 8 halves. Season each with salt and pepper.

In a wide, shallow bowl or a pie pan, mix the flour and garlic powder. Dredge each piece of chicken through the flour mixture to lightly coat both sides.

In a large skillet over medium-high, melt 1 tablespoon of the butter. Add 2 pieces of chicken and cook on each side for 3 minutes or until browned. Transfer to the prepared baking sheet. Set the baking sheet in the oven.

Repeat with the remaining chicken, using 1 tablespoon of butter per batch, adding each batch to the baking sheet in the oven as it finishes.

Return the skillet to the heat. Add the red peppers, onion, garlic, thyme, and capers. Sauté until the peppers are soft, about 5 minutes.

Add the wine, then use a wooden spoon to scrape the pan to release any bits stuck to the bottom. When the liquid has reduced by half, season with salt and pepper.

Serve the chicken topped with the sauce.

To keep bread from getting soggy: First, toast it. Second, put a layer of fat between it and the other ingredients (in this case, mayo).

Are you a heat fiend? Pack some jalapeño slices, too.

A tender bagel (such as potato or salt) is awesome for building a cold chicken sandwich. Pile on some lettuce, tomato slices, and honey mustard.

This sandwich combination—a riff on the classic Cubano—is crazy good. Just do it. Cold chicken cutlet, sliced cheddar cheese, deli ham, dill pickle slices, and mayo.

ONE DINNER
TWO LUNCHES

Mashed carrots? That's right. Make them for dinner or just prep a small portion for lunch. Either way, all you do is steam them until very tender, then mash with salt, pepper, and butter.

Want a low-carb solution to your chip cravings? Hunks of fennel bulb. Seriously. Pair them with a packet of guacamole to squeeze on. Unbelievably good.

SNACK P
Classic Guac
PORTANT: Keep
NT 2 OZ (5/g)

CUBANO WITH A TWIST

CHICKEN BAGEL SANDWICH

AROUND-THE-WORLD CHICKEN SALAD

Toss chopped leftover chicken (or grab a rotisserie) and chopped celery with low-fat sour cream spiked with whatever seasoning blend gets you going—Jamaican jerk rub, Cajun seasonings, Italian herbs, Chinese 5-spice, curry powder. Eat a different "cuisine" every day of the week.

Spike purchased hummus with chunks of salami. It's a Turkish thing. It's a crazy good thing.

vitaminwater zero
naturally sweetened

Nutrition Facts

When a fruit is in season, the best way to pack it is straight up.

Toss chunks of cold cooked chicken with a blend of low-fat sour cream and barbecue sauce. Perfect for spooning into purchased crepes.

Tabbouleh salad (find it premade next to the hummus) is easily doctored with extra veggies.

CHICKEN SALAD CREPES

I had no idea that teaching my son how to make a quick dinner by splitting open whole chickens before roasting them could help him in science class. Parker's third-grade class was studying vertebrates and invertebrates, and for homework he needed to classify a list of animals, indicating whether or not each had a backbone.

"The chicken is easy," he said. "I know they have backbones."

"How do you know that?"

"Because I've watched you spank-cock them."

Something may have gotten lost in the translation on that one.

Not that having him say it correctly—spatchcocking—would sound much better on the playground. It's a funny word for kids to say. It's also fun to gross them out a bit by teaching them how to do it.

But it's worth it either way. Cutting the backbone out of a chicken so it can be spread flat is such an easy trick for speeding up roast chicken. I often do two at once just to have the leftovers. There's a whole lot of spank-cocking going on in our house. (See page 36 for directions.)

ROSEMARY-GARLIC
ROASTED CHICKEN
WITH DRIPPING GOOD NEW POTATOES

Start to finish: **1 HOUR 15 MINUTES (15 MINUTES ACTIVE)**

Servings: **4 MAINS, PLUS LEFTOVERS**

Splitting open a chicken by cutting out its backbone—technically called spatch-cocking—dramatically cuts roasting time. In this recipe, I save even more time by cutting each chicken completely in half. The smaller pieces cook faster than whole birds. Add gobs of flavor with fresh rosemary, garlic, and black pepper and you end up with an amazing dinner—and equally impressive leftovers—with just a few minutes of hands-on time.

After dinner is the best time to salvage the leftovers from a roasted chicken. The meat is cool enough to handle, but still tender enough to easily separate from the bones.

2 pounds new potatoes, quartered

8 cloves garlic, minced

Three 8-inch sprigs fresh rosemary, minced

2 tablespoons kosher salt

1 tablespoon ground black pepper

½ cup olive oil

Two 4- to 5-pound whole chickens

Heat the oven to 475°F. Spritz a rimmed baking sheet with cooking spray. Arrange the potatoes in an even layer on the baking sheet. Set aside.

In a small bowl, mix together the garlic, rosemary, salt, pepper, and olive oil.

One at a time, set the chickens breast down on the cutting board. Use sturdy kitchen shears to cut down the length of the backbone on both sides. Discard the backbone.

Turn each bird breast up. Use the shears to cut between the breasts, first through the meat, then a second pass through the bone beneath, creating a total of 4 halves of chicken.

One at a time, rub the garlic-rosemary mixture over and under the skin of each chicken half. Set the chickens, skin side up, on top of the potatoes.

Roast for 1 hour or until the thickest part of the chickens reaches 165°F. Remove the chickens from the oven and let rest 5 minutes before carving.

BBQ pulled chicken! Mix shredded leftover chicken with bottled barbecue sauce, then keep it hot in a thermos. Pack the bun on the side.

Mango and star fruit are easy to jazz up with a pinch of cayenne. Don't do heat? A sprinkle of white balsamic or cider vinegar is great, too.

LunchBots

The ubiquitous string cheese is way more interesting when wrapped in prosciutto. For adults, add an asparagus spear to the bundle.

Shredded leftover chicken tossed with a few tablespoons of coconut milk, a splash of lime juice, and a bit of chopped fresh cilantro becomes a Thai-influenced sandwich filling. Add hot sauce for zip.

ONE DINNER

TWO LUNCHES

Snapea Crisps: all the crunch of a potato chip, but the nutritional street cred of a veggie.

Dress up baby carrots with a drizzle of toasted sesame oil, sesame seeds, and a pinch of kosher salt.

BBQ PULLED CHICKEN SANDWICH

THAI CHICKEN SANDWICH

ROASTED CHICKEN THIGHS
WITH GARLICKY WHITE BEANS
AND TOMATOES

Start to finish: **30 MINUTES**

Servings: **4 MAINS, PLUS LEFTOVERS**

A high-flavor one-pan meal that comes together in no time. Feel free to add more roasting-friendly vegetables to the dish.

Two 15-ounce cans white beans, drained

1 pint cherry tomatoes

4 cloves garlic, minced

3 tablespoons olive oil, divided

2 tablespoons chopped fresh rosemary

Kosher salt and ground black pepper

2 pounds boneless, skinless chicken thighs

1 lemon, cut into wedges

Heat the oven to 425°F. Line a rimmed baking sheet with foil, then coat it with cooking spray.

On the baking sheet, combine the beans, cherry tomatoes, garlic, 1 tablespoon of the olive oil, the rosemary, and a bit of salt and pepper. Mix well, then arrange in an even layer.

Nestle the chicken thighs into the beans and tomatoes; it's OK for the chicken to cover them. Drizzle the chicken with the remaining 2 tablespoons of oil, then season with salt and pepper.

Squeeze the lemon wedges over everything. Roast for 20 to 25 minutes, until the chicken reaches 165°F.

Serve the chicken with the bean and tomato mixture spooned over it.

Leftover beans (and veggies) can be heated and packed solo in a thermos.

Aioli makes raw veggies irresistible. Don't feel like making it from scratch? Find it jarred next to the mayo. And remember, a little goes a long way.

ONE
DINNER
TWO
LUNCHES

Make it even better with a sprinkle of cumin, sesame seeds, and oregano.

Got leftover cold chicken and beans? Add some cheese, carrots, and greens, and you've got a pretty killer chef's salad.

MIDDLE EASTERN CHICKEN AND HUMMUS SANDWICH

CHEF'S SALAD

SHEPHERD'S PIE

CHICKEN PAPRIKASH WRAP

No time to bake up a shepherd's pie? No need to. Nuke leftover mashed or roasted potatoes. Nuke canned corn kernels. Nuke some meat (anything from deli turkey to rotisserie chicken will do). Layer it in a thermos. Done.

A very round salad—cherry tomatoes plus watermelon and apples scooped with a melon baller— needs just a splash of vinegar, salt, and pepper.

Blend low-fat sour cream, smoked paprika, and black pepper until yummy, then toss with chopped cooked chicken.

Got cherry tomatoes and bread? You got crostini. Slice the tomatoes, toss with salt, pepper, olive oil, and balsamic vinegar. Pack some toasted bread separately. Assemble at lunch.

Eat almonds solo as a snack, or use them to add crunch to the salad.

BLUE DIAMOND NATURAL
Oven Roasted Almonds
Calories
Sea Salt

FAST
& EASY

SUSHI

The same seaweed used to wrap sushi also makes awesome (addictive) chips. Check the natural foods section for this ultrahealthy snack.

Brown apples, but in a good way. Brush apple wedges with cider vinegar and sesame oil, then sprinkle with sugar and brown briefly in a skillet.

Purchased sushi: the ultimate feel-good convenience. Raw seafood turns you off? Stick with vegetables. And brown rice makes it whole grain.

1-MINUTE MAC AND CHEESE

Toss leftover cooked pasta (any shape) in a saucepan with crème fraîche, grated Parmesan, and a splash of hot sauce. Once it's hot and melty, pop it in a thermos.

For something acidic to balance the cheese and meat, pickled green beans are a savory-sweet choice you can find at the grocer alongside the pickles.

Sliced salami can be eaten solo, or added to the mac and cheese.

2-MINUTE STIR-FRY

Leftover rice
(or a packet of heat-and-eat)
plus a what-have-you of veggies
becomes a 2-minute stir-fry.
Dump everything in the skillet you
used to cook breakfast.
Once it starts to get hot, crack an
egg into the center and stir like
mad. When the egg is cooked,
splash it with soy sauce,
then pop it into
a thermos.

Save
chopsticks
from takeout
or find some in
your grocer's
international
aisle.

POTSTICKERS

Frozen chicken or vegetable potstickers are ready for the thermos after just 2 minutes in the microwave.

Salty. Sweet. Creamy. Crunchy. Soft goat cheese topped with all-fruit grape jelly with pretzels for dipping. The combination will blow you away.

Or if you used a skillet at breakfast, heat and crisp them in that.

Don't forget some soy sauce or sweet-and-sour sauce for dunking.

COTTAGE CHEESE COMEBACK

'70s flashback? No way. Cottage cheese has had an artisanal makeover and it's delicious paired with funky crisp breads.

Turkey jerky isn't just fun to say! It's also a delicious lean protein that fills you up and has just 60 calories per serving. And check out bison and salmon jerky, too.

Fresh berries would be fine, but strawberry jam is fabulous.

LunchBots

1-MINUTE SOLUTIONS

Some mornings, even easy lunches are too difficult. Don't fight it and don't feel bad. Here are some lunch ideas you can pack in a snap.

Use prepackaged hummus or peanut butter for dipping vegetables. If it keeps you on schedule in the morning, the convenience is worth the extra expense.

PB&J feels fresh when made on graham crackers.

Keep a box of cheesy cracker sandwiches on hand.

DIY NACHOS

No heavy lifting here.

Flan? Why not? After all, if you're going to pack a convenience treat, might as well rise above the basic pudding cup.

PEEL CORNERS

HOLLY
AMERICAN
GUACAMOLE

CAL

ACK PACKS
ssic Guacamole

Keep refrigerated to maintain safety. ⓤ

Serve. Size 1 pouch (57g). Servings 1 pouch. Amount Per
00). Cal. Fat Cal. 90. Total Fat 10g (15% DV). Sat. Fat 1.5g
g. Polyunsat. fat 1g. Monounsat. fat 7g. Cholest. 0mg
70mg (7% DV). Potassium 330mg (9% DV). Total Carb.
g (12% DV). Sugars 2g. Protein 1g. Vitamin A (2% DV).
Calcium (0% DV). Iron (2% DV). Vitamin B6 (10% DV).
cent Daily Values) are based on a 2,000 calorie diet.

ss Avocados, Jalapeño Purée (white vinegar,
, salt), Dehydrated Onion, Salt, Granulated Garlic

CO   GLUTEN FREE

.com
ed Foods
. Saginaw,

EZE B
D

DIY BAKED POTATO BAR

Salty, crunchy, cheesy, and wildly addictive. Who knew kale could taste so good? Kale chips are cheap to make or easy to buy.

Having baked potatoes for dinner? Bake an extra for a thermos-friendly lunch that can be topped with whatever leftovers you have (packed separately or in the same thermos). Beef stew, chili, and baked beans are fine choices. Ditto for any cooked veggies.

To make your own kale chips, cut fresh kale into large pieces (discard the stems), toss with olive oil and seasonings (salt and garlic powder are nice), then bake at 350°F until lightly browned and crispy.

KALE CHIPS

MEANWHILE, ZESTY NACH

POW!

A REAL NUTRIENT SUPERHERO OF A SNACK AND A YUMMY ALTERNATI TO TRADITIONAL CHIPS

EXCELLENT SOURCE OF VITAMIN A
GOOD SOURCE OF FIBER, VITAMIN C
AND CALCIUM AND IRON

2 OZ (57g)

1-MINUTE PASTA CARBONARA

A few spoons of canned pumpkin and a pinch of pumpkin pie spice mixed with a fat-free chocolate Greek yogurt become an instant, healthy pumpkin pie pudding.

Want crust with your pie? Crumble some graham crackers over it.

Toss some chopped ham or cooked bacon in a skillet with a splash of oil and leftover pasta. As soon as it's hot, take it off the heat and stir in an egg (yes, raw) and some grated Parmesan. Stir until saucy. Salt, pepper, and done.

Raw egg not your style? Use sour cream, crème fraîche, or even plain Greek yogurt instead.

1-MINUTE COLD SESAME NOODLE SALAD

BIG-FLAVOR SALAD

Toss leftover pasta (whatever shape) with tahini (sesame seed butter), soy sauce, vinegar, maybe a splash of hot sauce, and sesame seeds. If you want, add veggies. Done.

No tahini (it's sold alongside the peanut butter and in the international aisle)? Any nut butter can be substituted.

1 can (artichokes) + 1 handful (cherry tomatoes) + 1 slice (baguette) + 1 splash (Caesar dressing) = easy, big-flavor salad

Ch-ch-ch-ch-chia! Hipster drink companies add them to juice, but you can use them to make pudding. Add ¼ cup of chia seeds to a cup of vanilla almond milk with a bit of honey and cinnamon. Stir, refrigerate overnight. That's it.

Yet another convenience item you can feel good about. Check near the deli counter for mozzarella sticks ready-wrapped in prosciutto and pepperoni.

FEEL-GOOD CONVENIENCE

If you shop smart, there are plenty of convenience foods you can feel good about packing. Small packets of Italian meats and cheese are a protein-rich start.

Baguette slices can be combined with the meat and cheese for DIY pizzas, or used with peanut butter and apple slices for a side.

Unlike packaged lunches marketed to kids, these meats and cheeses are real foods with real flavor.

1-MINUTE FETTUCCINE ALFREDO

Real Alfredo sauce has just 3 ingredients—butter, Parmesan, and black pepper. That makes it an easy, awesome lunch box fix.

Just add low-fat sour cream and fresh dill to turn purchased seasoned beets into a healthy, sweet side.

Heat leftover pasta in a saucepan with a splash of oil. As soon as it's hot, add butter (at least 1 tablespoon), grated Parmesan (at least ½ cup), and pepper (as much as you can handle), then toss until melty. Now get it into a thermos.

CATCH
OF THE DAY

SHRIMP COCKTAIL

The easiest—and most decadent—lunch ever. Shrimp cocktail isn't just for party appetizers. It's also lean and filling. Buy the shrimp cooked and peeled at the seafood counter.

Fruit, prepackaged and ready to eat. Sometimes convenience is worth a little extra.

Gotta love a 4-ingredient salad that packs this much flavor: cooked shrimp, chickpeas, and chopped fresh parsley over arugula.

Want to take it in a different direction? Sub cilantro for the parsley, add diced red onion, and use lime juice instead of lemon. Avocado wouldn't be a bad addition, either.

For dressing, just a squeeze of lemon juice, salt, and pepper.

LEMON-PAPRIKA
ROASTED SALMON

Start to finish: **30 MINUTES**

Servings: **4 MAINS, PLUS LEFTOVERS**

This simple recipe for roasted salmon packs gobs of flavor for little effort. The natural oils in the fish intensify the seasonings. This recipe also can be used for smaller fillets or salmon steaks. You'll just need to watch it as it cooks and adjust the time accordingly.

FOR THE SALMON:

1 teaspoon **smoked paprika**

1 teaspoon **garlic powder**

1 teaspoon **kosher salt**

½ teaspoon **ground black pepper**

Zest and juice of 1 lemon

2 tablespoons **olive oil, divided**

2½-pound **salmon fillet**

FOR THE GREEN BEANS:

1 pound **green beans, trimmed**

3 cloves **garlic, minced**

1 teaspoon **kosher salt**

¼ cup **chopped Marcona almonds**

Heat the oven to 400°F. Line a rimmed baking sheet with foil, then coat it lightly with cooking spray.

In a small bowl, mix together the paprika, garlic powder, salt, pepper, and lemon zest. Add 1 tablespoon of the olive oil, then mix well.

Set the salmon on the prepared pan. Gently rub the oil-seasoning mixture over the salmon. Set aside.

In a medium bowl, toss the green beans with the remaining 1 tablespoon of olive oil, the garlic, and salt. Arrange the green beans around the salmon.

Roast for 25 minutes or until the fish flakes easily when tested with a fork. Sprinkle the green beans with the almonds. Drizzle the lemon juice over the salmon.

A fresh way to get your greens: "pickled" cucumber salad. Use a veggie peeler to shave a cuke into ribbons, then toss with seasoned rice vinegar and sesame seeds.

This is one of the easiest lunches to pack. Think big. Think kitchen sink: Pile on greens, whatever leftover or raw vegetables you have, then top with leftover salmon and something crunchy, like nuts.

ONE DINNER
TWO LUNCHES

Soy sauce and rice vinegar complete the sushi flavor vibe.

Salmon doesn't need fancy dressings. Try a splash of sesame oil and vinegar.

No rolling, no fuss. Pack leftover salmon on top of leftover (or a bag of heat-and-eat) rice, then crumble a sheet of nori (seaweed sushi wrap) over it. Eat it cold or hot.

No leftover salmon? Smoked salmon is great in salads.

DECONSTRUCTED SUSHI

MONSTER SALAD

LOBSTER ROLL

Bake a batch of your favorite muffins in a mini muffin tin during the weekend. Freeze two or three to a bag, then pop them in the lunch box frozen. They'll be perfect by lunch.

Be decadent and have a lobster roll. But also make it cheap and easy: Use imitation lobster (find it at the seafood counter), mayo, celery, and a splash of hot sauce.

Lettuce helps keep bread from getting soggy when your sandwich has a moist filling. Dressed with lime juice, an avocado (and corn) salad won't turn brown.

Lime
Italian Sparkling
Mineral Water
16.9 FL OZ (500mL)

WHOLE FOODS

SUSHI SALAD

Green salads are boring. Sushi salads? Much more exciting. Toss leftover rice (or tear open a package of heat-and-eat rice) with cooked shrimp or crab (frozen works—just thaw overnight), diced avocado, rice vinegar, and sesame seeds.

Asian grocers are jammed with sweet treats made from rice and beans, such as these mochi cakes, also called *daifuku*.

BAKED BREADED
HADDOCK

Start to finish: **30 MINUTES**

Servings: **4 MAINS, PLUS LEFTOVERS**

The "special sauce"—ketchup, mustard, and mayo!—brushed over the haddock keeps it incredibly moist, even for leftovers the next day.

Don't care for haddock? This recipe works just as well with cod, tilapia, catfish, red snapper, whatever.

½ cup **all-purpose flour**

1 teaspoon **kosher salt**

½ teaspoon **ground black pepper**

2 **eggs**

2 pounds **haddock fillets**

¼ cup **ketchup**

¼ cup **mustard**

¼ cup **mayonnaise**

1½ cups **panko breadcrumbs**

Heat the oven to 425°F. Line a rimmed baking sheet with foil, then coat it lightly with cooking spray.

In a pie pan or wide, shallow bowl, mix together the flour, salt, and pepper. In a second pan or bowl, whisk the eggs.

One fillet at a time, dredge the haddock through the flour mixture, lightly coating it on all sides, then through the egg, then again through the flour.

Arrange the coated haddock on the prepared baking sheet.

In a small bowl, stir together the ketchup, mustard, and mayonnaise. Use a basting brush or spoon to spread the mixture thickly over the top of each piece of fish, coating all the way to the edge. Use all of the mayonnaise mixture.

Sprinkle the panko evenly over each fillet, spritz the tops with cooking spray, then bake for 15 minutes or until the fish flakes easily at the center.

Fish sandwiches are great cold. Want it hot? Nuke the fish, then pack it on its own in a thermos. Assemble when ready to eat.

Leftover breaded fish fillets become a fast-food knockoff with just a bun, lettuce, and some tartar sauce.

Snack pouches aren't limited to traditional snack foods.

ONE DINNER **TWO** LUNCHES

Find sweet pickled Peppadew peppers at the olive bar. They beg to be stuffed with feta cheese.

Cheese and crackers never lose their appeal. Especially when you pair an aged cheddar with strawberry jam.

Smoked fish—such as haddock or salmon—is meaty and filling without being heavy. A smear of cream cheese or crème fraîche and you're good to go. Wanna get fancy? Add a squirt of lemon.

FISH FILLET SANDWICH

A SMOKY SEAFOOD LUNCH

INSTANT SEAFOOD SALAD

SHRIMP QUESADILLAS

Sweet-and-sour mango slaw = thinly sliced mango tossed with golden raisins, vinegar, sesame oil, and a tiny sprinkle of sugar.

Tortillas + cheese + sliced cooked shrimp + the frying pan you used to make breakfast = shrimp quesadillas. This works for just about any cooked and thinly sliced meat, too.

A fresh approach to cukes! Cheese and crackers, minus the crackers.

Just add mayo to leftover cooked shrimp for seafood salad. Paprika or a splash of hot sauce is nice, too.

Protein salad! Top hummus with diced cucumbers, cherry tomatoes, and black pepper. No dressing needed.

BREAKFAST
FOR LUNCH

OATMEAL-TURNED-LUNCH

Making oatmeal for breakfast? Make too much, pop it in a thermos, and top it with a bit of peanut butter and jelly for a warm, sweet, and filling lunch.

Grapes and goat cheese belong together, even on bread. Got more time? Roast the grapes first. Or toss them in the skillet after breakfast.

SCRAMBLED EGGS FOR LUNCH

A splash of hot sauce would be delicious, too. If you're a heat fiend, grab a tiny "travel" bottle of hot sauce to keep in your lunch box.

Having scrambled eggs for breakfast? Make extra and pop them in a thermos. At lunch, squeeze some guacamole on toasted bread, then top with warm scrambled eggs.

Ham salad doesn't have to be unhealthy. Toss cherry tomatoes, canned corn kernels, and chopped leftover ham (or any meat) with vinaigrette.

BROWN SUGAR–CINNAMON APPLES

Done with breakfast? Don't wash the skillet just yet. Use it to make brown sugar–cinnamon apples.

Also good on yogurt or granola.

Sauté peeled apple wedges, cinnamon, and butter until lightly browned, then add a splash of lemon juice and brown sugar. Pack in a thermos to keep warm, then spoon over leftover pancakes, waffles, or French toast.

Pineapple, cheese, and ham? Hawaiian kebabs!

HAM AND CHEESE MUFFIN CUPS

There is nothing wrong with mixing cultures. Pair whole-wheat matzo (giant crackers) with Spanish manchego cheese and guava paste (thick jam).

Easy, funky, and delicious: Coat a muffin tin with cooking spray, press a slice of deli ham into each cup, then fill each with an egg and cheese. Bake until set. Don't hesitate to add chopped veggies, too.

WHOLE-WHEAT
PANCAKES

Start to finish: **20 MINUTES**

Makes: **20 PANCAKES**

Whether for dinner or breakfast, I never make just enough pancakes. They freeze so well and reheat so easily, I always make a double batch. Pancakes also are wonderfully versatile. I like to use the leftovers in place of bread for a fresh take on an otherwise same-old sandwich.

White whole-wheat flour is sold right alongside the all-purpose. It looks and tastes like white flour, but has all the nutrition of whole-grain.

This recipe (already doubled for your convenience) is just lightly sweet, so the pancakes work well with sweet or savory toppings.

2 cups white whole-wheat flour

2 tablespoons sugar

4 teaspoons baking powder

½ teaspoon kosher salt

2 eggs

2 cups milk

3 tablespoons canola or vegetable oil

In a large bowl, whisk together the flour, sugar, baking powder, and salt.

In a medium bowl, whisk together the eggs, milk, and oil. Pour the wet ingredients into the dry, then stir until thoroughly blended.

Heat a nonstick skillet over medium heat. When the pan is hot, add batter in ¼-cup portions, leaving room for the pancakes to spread.

Cook the pancakes for 2 to 3 minutes, then flip and brown on the other side. Repeat with the remaining batter.

If desired, cooked pancakes can be kept warm in a 200°F oven while the rest are prepared.

Keep fruit from browning by tossing it with a splash of lemon juice just before packing.

Continue the breakfast theme with ham and eggs.

A batch of tapioca pudding will last the week and is a great source of dairy. Use the easy recipe on the box, but cut the sugar by half and sprinkle with fruit for a feel-good treat.

ONE DINNER
TWO LUNCHES

After threading fruit onto skewers, use kitchen shears to snip off the sharp tips to prevent Zorro from attacking his lunchmates.

From breakfast to bread: slather leftover pancakes with cream cheese and jam.

Peanut butter on one, chocolate-hazelnut spread on another, healthy strawberries on both, and whole grains all around.

PANCAKE SANDWICH

PEANUT BUTTER AND CHOCOLATE-HAZELNUT PANCAKES

CREPES-ON-THE-GO

Leftover or purchased crepes fold and pack easily for topping with fruit later.

Did your morning start with sausage or bacon? Cook a little extra to round out your lunch.

Sweeten vanilla Greek yogurt with maple syrup for an easy sauce.

NO-COOK OATMEAL PUDDING

Chicken salad doesn't have to be an artery clogger. Sub vinaigrette for the mayo.

Plain cukes are dull. Turn them into "sushi" bites with ham, a whole-wheat tortilla, and a smear of cream cheese to seal the rolls shut.

It's so easy, so delicious, and so good for you. Mix ½ cup old-fashioned rolled oats with ¼ cup Greek yogurt and ¼ cup milk. Add cinnamon, a bit of brown sugar, and fruit, then refrigerate overnight. It's ready to pack and eat by morning.

SCRAMBLED EGG WRAP

Scrambling eggs for breakfast? Scramble a few spare, then layer with ham and cheese for an easy wrap.

While you've got the pan on the heat, toss in some pineapple rings and a tiny pat of butter. Cinnamon is nice, too.

R.W. KNUDSEN
FAMILY

Organic pear

juice from concentrate

100% juice

✓ 100% RDI*
✓ vitamin C
✓ good source of calcium

QUICHE FOR LUNCH

Pack leftover purchased quiche in a jar thermos if you want it hot, or just pack it cold. It's delicious either way.

Whipped low-fat cream cheese blended with orange zest, cinnamon, and a splash of honey, make a fine dip for whole-grain pretzels and banana chips.

Prosciutto-wrapped melon slices aren't just for dinner parties.

ROASTED
HAM STEAKS
WITH SAVORY HASH BROWNS

Start to finish: **1 HOUR**
(15 MINUTES ACTIVE)

Servings: **4 MAINS, PLUS LEFTOVERS**

Fast, easy, and versatile—that's my kind of ham.

3 tablespoons olive oil

1 teaspoon garlic powder

1 teaspoon kosher salt

½ teaspoon smoked paprika

½ teaspoon ground black pepper

30-ounce bag frozen shredded potatoes (hash browns)

5 ounces (about 1½ cups) shredded carrots

3½ tablespoons maple syrup

1½ tablespoons Dijon mustard

Splash of hot sauce

Three 12-ounce ham steaks

Heat the oven to 475°F. Line two rimmed baking sheets with foil, then coat with cooking spray.

In a large bowl, whisk together the olive oil, garlic powder, salt, smoked paprika, and pepper. Add the potatoes and carrots, then toss to mix and coat evenly.

Transfer the potato-carrot mixture to one baking sheet, arranging in an even layer. Spritz the top with cooking spray. Roast for 30 minutes.

Meanwhile, in a small bowl, whisk together the maple syrup, mustard, and hot sauce.

Arrange the ham steaks on the second baking sheet. Spoon or brush half of the mustard mixture over them.

When the potatoes have roasted for 30 minutes, add the ham steaks to the oven. Roast for 10 minutes, then flip the steaks, brush with the remaining mustard sauce, and roast for another 10 minutes.

Increase the oven to broil and cook for another 2 minutes.

Serve the steaks with the crisped potato-carrot hash browns.

Leftover ham + canned corn + sliced cherry tomatoes + chopped romaine + sliced hard-boiled eggs + cheese = an awesome Cobb salad.

Fast-food-style ham-and-egg breakfast sandwiches can be an anytime meal. If you want it warm, pop it in a wide-mouthed thermos.

ONE DINNER
TWO LUNCHES

Dried fruit makes any salad better.

Mini bell peppers become poppers when filled with anything from hummus to goat cheese to purchased tabbouleh.

COBB SALAD

HAM-AND-EGG BREAKFAST SANDWICH FOR LUNCH

INSTANT HASH

Keep a bag of shredded potatoes in the freezer. Combine them with leftover meat (or use a purchased rotisserie chicken) for a few minutes in a skillet and you've got a near instant hash.

Cheddar cheese and apples are a classic New England combination. So butter some toast, then top with cinnamon and cheddar. Toast until melty, then cool and cut.

Don't forget the applesauce for dunking.

R.W. KNUDSEN
FAMILY
Organic
Apple

WAFFLE OPEN-FACED SANDWICH

Break out of your same-old-saltine routine. Mix it up by experimenting with cracker varieties, such as seeded or rice crackers.

A fresh take on the open-faced sandwich: fresh fruit and ricotta on a toasted waffle. Mascarpone or soft goat cheese are great, too.

Creamed honey + Dijon mustard = delicious dip for fresh veggies.

PANCAKE, BACON, HAM, AND CHEESE

Fruit wedges fit into lunch containers more easily than full pieces.

Feeling indulgent? Add some leftover breakfast bacon to a pancake grilled ham and cheese.

Who needs milk? A favorite dry cereal mixed with dried fruit becomes a satisfying trail mix.

SANDWICHES
& THINGS
BREADY

PEANUT BUTTER AND FRUIT BURRITO

MEATBALL HERO

Fig-almond cake (you'll find it next to the good cheeses at the grocer) is a classic pairing for cheeses and cured meats in Italy and Portugal.

Hunks of Parmesan beg to be dunked in honey.

Just smear PB over a whole-wheat tortilla, then fill with a banana and strips of apple or pear. Roll tightly, folding the ends in.

Pack the meatballs in a thermos so they stay hot AND won't make the bread soggy. A side of cheddar cheese and your sub is good to go.

Pan-fry frozen meatballs—or faux meat meatballs—after frying your breakfast egg.

Fruit and feta. Better together.

SMALL SANDWICHES

Multiple small sandwiches are way more fun than one big one. Mini croissants with ham and cheese are a fine way to go, but so are mini bagels.

No time for a spoon? Drink your yogurt as kefir, a fruity cultured yogurt drink that packs plenty of protein and probiotics. Or try an Indian lassi, which also is yogurt-based. Most grocers sell a bunch of varieties alongside the yogurt.

Nuts can be way more than salted or plain. Check out cocoa powder, chili, and other funky varieties.

It takes just one power ingredient like Parmesan (or kalamata olives or Peppadew peppers or crumbled bacon) to make a dull salad delicious.

PIZZA SUSHI

Baby kale, golden raisins, and goat cheese. Perfectly simple. Simply delicious.

Soy sauce doesn't work for this sushi, but marinara does.

Not exactly a chocolate fountain, but who's going to complain about fruit dunked in chocolate yogurt?

A layer of salty, crunchy pretzels puts an otherwise basic peanut butter sandwich over the top. Baked potato chips would be tasty, too!

Pizza sushi? That's right. Spread cream cheese on a whole-wheat tortilla, then layer pepperoni and jarred roasted red peppers over it. Roll it up and cut it.

PRETZEL PEANUT BUTTER SANDWICH

STEAMED DUMPLINGS

Whether leftovers from last night's takeout or grabbed from the grocer's freezer section, steamed dumplings are easy to heat and delicious to eat.

Asian restaurants often serve orange slices at the end of the meal. You can have them anytime.

Best dipping sauce ever is also the easiest: mix equal parts seasoned rice vinegar and soy sauce with a splash of hot sauce.

POLAR TONIC WATER

SINCE 1882
CONTAINS QUININE

BREADED AND BAKED
CHICKEN TENDERS
WITH SWEET-AND-SOUR SAUCE

Start to finish: **45 MINUTES
(20 MINUTES ACTIVE)**

Servings: **4 MAINS,
PLUS LEFTOVERS**

Chicken tenders . . . the bane of parenting. Except these aren't the processed taste-less variety from giant freezer bags. These are good enough for kids and adults.

It's always cheaper to buy boneless, skinless chicken breasts and slice them into strips. But to save time, you can buy breasts already sliced into tenders. You also can use turkey tenderloin for this recipe.

FOR THE CHICKEN:

1 cup **all-purpose flour**

1 teaspoon **kosher salt**

½ teaspoon **ground black pepper**

4 **eggs**

3 tablespoons **Dijon mustard**

4 cups **panko breadcrumbs**

2 teaspoons **chili powder**

4½ pounds boneless,
skinless **chicken breasts**

FOR THE SWEET-AND-SOUR SAUCE:

½ cup **rice vinegar**
(**cider vinegar** can be substituted)

⅔ cup packed **brown sugar**

2 tablespoons **apricot jam**

2 tablespoons **ketchup**

2 teaspoons **soy sauce**

1 teaspoon **hot sauce**

1 tablespoon **cornstarch**

Heat the oven to 375°F. Line two rimmed baking sheets with foil, then coat them lightly with cooking spray.

In a wide, shallow bowl, mix the flour, salt, and pepper. In a second bowl, whisk together the eggs and mustard. In a third, mix the breadcrumbs and chili powder.

One at a time, lay each chicken breast flat on the cutting board. Slice lengthwise into 3 or 4 strips.

One at a time, place each strip in the flour, lightly coating both sides. Next, dip the tender in the egg, coating it, but shaking off any excess. Finally, dip in the breadcrumb mixture, coating it evenly. Place the finished tender on the baking sheet. Repeat with the remaining tenders.

Bake for 25 to 30 minutes, until lightly golden.

Meanwhile, prepare the sweet-and-sour sauce: In a small saucepan over medium heat, combine the vinegar, sugar, jam, ketchup, soy sauce, and hot sauce. Bring to a simmer. In a small glass, mix the cornstarch and 2 tablespoons water. Add to the sauce. Simmer for another 2 minutes or until slightly thickened.

Not only are rice cakes whole grain, they also don't taste like cardboard anymore.

Carrots and hummus passé? Pimp your hummus with hot sauce, BBQ sauce (seriously!), chopped sun-dried tomatoes, or balsamic vinegar.

A melon baller makes simple work of apples and—go figure—melons. A splash of lemon juice keeps the apples looking fresh.

Salads don't need lots of ingredients, just lots of contrast. Try sweet strawberries, peppery spinach, and crunchy almonds.

ONE DINNER
TWO LUNCHES

Do it hot. Do it cold. Either way, chicken and waffles (with a creamy dressing, such as blue cheese) simply belong together.

Wrap it or slap it on slices. Leftover chicken tenders plus veggies and bottled Caesar dressing make for a salad sandwich that's easy to get a handle on.

WAFFLE CHICKEN SANDWICH

CHICKEN CAESAR SANDWICH

POPOVERS

These are an easy double-duty dish. Make a batch in the morning (you can even make the batter the night before). Enjoy fresh from the oven for breakfast.

Then pack the leftovers along with ham, cheese, and jam for lunch.

Popovers:
In a blender, blitz 1 tablespoon olive oil, 2 eggs, 1 cup milk, 1 teaspoon sugar, 1 teaspoon thyme, pinch of salt, and 1 cup all-purpose flour. Dump into a muffin tin or popover pan (fill each cup ¾ full). Bake for 20 minutes at 400°F.

Depending on the size of your pan, this recipe makes 4 to 8 popovers.

THANKSGIVING SANDWICH

Nuke leftover mashed potatoes, pop them in a thermos, then add a pat of butter to keep them nice and moist.

Deli turkey slices + cheese + sliced apple + a dollop of cranberry sauce = delicious.

Need to atone for buttery mashed potatoes? Have some carrot and celery sticks, too (though I'd include low-fat sour cream with bacon for dipping).

CUCUMBERS AS BREAD

Fat-free Greek yogurt is so much richer than regular yogurt. And real fruit is so much tastier (and healthier) than fruit-on-the-bottom.

Couscous is one of the easiest grains to cook. Combine 1 cup couscous with 2 cups boiling water. Cover and let sit for 5 minutes, then fluff. Be sure to make extra. It freezes well.

Couscous tossed with a what-have-you of roasted or steamed veggies makes a healthy and filling salad. Drizzle with vinaigrette or Caesar dressing.

Up the appeal of cukes by filling them with your favorite sandwich fixings.

After you grill your sandwich, toss broccoli florets and olive oil into the same skillet over low heat. Cover and walk away for a few minutes. Pop into a thermos with a bit of cheese.

An easy grilled sandwich you can make in the same skillet you cooked breakfast in: cheese, apple slices, and deli ham.

This method also makes delicious carrots, cauliflower, and peppers.

Just pile some baby spinach and crumbled feta between tortillas, then grill until melty.

Keep the Greek theme going with an easy feta-spiked salad. Don't get picky about ingredients—use what you have on hand.

For the calorie conscious, a little feta goes a long way. And low- and no-fat varieties are totally respectable.

GRILLED CHEESE WITH APPLE AND HAM

SPINACH AND FETA QUESADILLA

HONEY BRIE SANDWICH

Combining fresh and dried fruit creates a salad with tons of flavor and contrast. Slivered almonds add protein and crunch.

Yogurts are available in so many varieties—traditional, Greek, Icelandic, Australian. Don't even get me started on the flavors. Try something new.

siggi's
Icelandic style skyr
strained non-fat yogurt
Grade A | 0% milkfat

One of my son's favorites: sourdough smeared with Brie and topped with a drippy hunk of honeycomb (or just a drizzle of honey). Trust me (and him)— it's amazing.

HOISIN-RASPBERRY
PORK TENDERLOIN

Start to finish:
20 MINUTES (PLUS MARINATING)

Servings: **4 MAINS, PLUS LEFTOVERS**

This same recipe also is delicious with pork chops, but I like tenderloin because it's leaner and the leftovers are more versatile.

With just four ingredients, this recipe is easy to start in the morning to give the pork plenty of time to marinate. But if you're jammed for time, 30 minutes before dinner is fine, too.

Is it grilling season? Toss the marinated tenderloins on a medium-hot grill for about the same time.

1 cup hoisin sauce

½ cup all-fruit seedless raspberry jam

½ cup red wine

3¼ pounds pork tenderloin, trimmed of fat

In a large bowl, whisk together the hoisin, jam, and wine. Set aside.

Slice each tenderloin in half lengthwise, then cut each half in two crosswise to create 4 pieces from each tenderloin.

One at a time, place each piece between sheets of plastic wrap, then use a meat mallet or rolling pin to pound to an even thickness, about ½ inch.

Add the pork to the marinade, cover, and refrigerate until ready to cook. Aim for at least 30 minutes.

When ready to cook, heat the oven to 450°F. Set a wire rack over a rimmed baking sheet. Coat the rack with cooking spray.

Remove the meat from the marinade, reserving the marinade. Place the pork on the rack and roast for 5 minutes.

Flip the tenderloins, increase the heat to broil, and cook for another 5 minutes or until starting to brown.

Meanwhile, place the marinade in a small saucepan over medium-high heat and bring to a boil. Cook for 3 minutes or until reduced and thickened.

Let the pork rest for 5 minutes. Serve drizzled with the marinade.

Any cooked pork can become pulled pork. Just use two forks to shred the leftovers, then toss with your favorite barbecue sauce.

After you fry your egg for breakfast, shred leftover cooked pork and fry until crisp in the same pan for easy carnitas.

It takes just three items to add up to delicious: arugula, goat cheese, and dried cranberries.

The juice of fresh pineapples keeps bananas or apples from browning.

ONE DINNER

TWO LUNCHES

What do pickles and applesauce have in common? Cups of convenience you can feel good about.

For toasty corn tortillas, wrap them in foil and pop them in a warm oven for a few minutes. Then roll them up, foil and all, and pack them in a thermos.

PULLED PORK SANDWICH

CARNITAS

SPICY PEANUT TURKEY SANDWICH

Blend peanut butter and jarred salsa for instant spicy peanut sauce. Use as a sandwich spread with turkey, lettuce, and tomato.

Canned sauerkraut is just cabbage, salt, and water. Drain it, add chopped celery and bell peppers, then dress with mayo or bottled vinaigrette and a handful of golden raisins.

CORN QUESADILLAS

Keep the Mexican theme going by mixing leftover shredded chicken and salsa. Nuke it, then pop in a thermos and pair with tortilla chips.

Fill a whole-wheat tortilla with canned corn kernels, Mexican-style shredded cheese, and whatever else gets you going, such as sliced jalapeños. Toast in a dry or lightly oiled skillet.

NOT-SO-BASIC CHEESE SANDWICH

Jarred marinated mushrooms, oil-packed sun-dried tomatoes, and canned baby corn. An effortless salad that also would be delicious warmed and tossed with pasta and cheese.

Want to push it to toe-curling good? Slip in some prosciutto (or even just ham) and toast it.

There are so many ways to dress up a basic cheese sandwich. But for my money, soft goat cheese and fig jam are tops.

BRIE AND TOMATO BAGUETTE

CLASSIC GRILLED CHEESE

Never had kumquats? You are missing out. These tiny little explosions of citrus are conveniently eaten with their skin on. Include a pot of honey for dipping to balance the tartness.

What's good at Euro airport kiosks is good at lunch in America, too. The classic brie and tomato on baguette is simple, and simply delicious.

Having trouble packing a hot sandwich? Cut your grilled cheese into "soldiers" and pack them standing up in a thermos. This trick works for pizza, too!

Cranberry sauce isn't just for Thanksgiving. Spoon whole berry cranberry sauce and granola over yogurt.

PUFF PASTRY SWIRLS

Even when coated with caramel, popcorn is still a whole grain. And nothing says you can't doctor it with unsweetened dried fruit.

Puff pastry pinwheels aren't just party food. Thaw a sheet of puff pastry in the refrigerator overnight. In the morning, unfold, top with deli meat and cheese, then roll, slice, and bake the rounds at 400°F for 15 minutes.

No need to keep them warm. They're delicious at room temperature.

MAPLE PROSCIUTTO
AND EGG PIZZA

Start to finish: **30 MINUTES**

Servings: **4 MAINS (BAKE AN EXTRA PLAIN CRUST TO USE IN LUNCHES)**

Just trust me on this combination. It's like breakfast, on a pizza, but for dinner. And it's nothing short of breathtaking.

The point here is that when you make pizza at home (this or any recipe), buy an extra bag of dough, roll it out, and bake it without any toppings. The extra crust becomes your lunch building block the next day.

20-ounce ball pizza dough (buy an extra to bake for lunch leftovers)

2 tablespoons maple syrup

Red pepper flakes

2 cups (8 ounces) shredded mozzarella

6 ounces (about 12 slices) prosciutto, finely chopped

4 large eggs

Heat the oven to 400°F. Lightly coat two baking sheets with cooking spray.

Divide the dough into 4 pieces. On a lightly floured surface, roll out each piece until it is the size of a salad plate. Place 2 rounds on each baking sheet.

Brush a quarter of the maple syrup over the top of each piece of dough, then sprinkle each with red pepper flakes.

Top each pizza with about ¼ cup of the cheese, then divide the prosciutto among the pizzas. Finish each pizza with another ¼ cup of cheese.

Bake the pizzas for 8 minutes or until the crust is lightly puffed but not browned. Crack 1 egg into the center of each pizza, then bake for another 8 minutes or until the whites are cooked but the yolks are still runny.

LEFTOVERS
While the pizzas cook, divide an extra dough ball into 4 pieces and roll out. While eating, pop the plain crusts in the oven to bake. Cool them, then store at room temperature in plastic bags for use in lunches.

Use a round biscuit cutter to cut small "pizzas" out of a baked crust. Accompany with your favorite toppings, then just assemble as you eat.

Pizza can have a sweeter side, too. Cut leftover crust into wedges, then pack peanut butter or jam and whatever toppings inspire you. Banana chips, berries, coconut flakes, and raisins are a fine start.

ONE
DINNER

TWO
LUNCHES

The pizzas are meant to be eaten cold, but if you'd like them hot, nuke the sauce and pack it in a thermos.

DIY PIZZA LUNCH KITS

FRUITY PIZZA

ZUCCHINI AND RICOTTA SANDWICH

Slice zucchini paper thin, season with salt and pepper, then slap it on bread topped with ricotta cheese. A squeeze of lemon juice adds a nice touch, too.

Keep the zucchini theme rolling. Slice it in half, scoop out the seeds, then fill with cream cheese blended with hot sauce and fresh herbs.

PIMPED-OUT GRILLED CHEESE

While you've got the pan out, fry up a few sausages (chicken, pork, breakfast, whatever). Pop them in a thermos and accompany with a blend of Dijon mustard and maple syrup for dunking.

You could dedicate an entire book to pimping your grilled cheese. Chopped marinated olives, mushrooms, and sun-dried tomatoes are a fine place to start.

MEATBALL WRAP

Purchased tzatziki (cucumber-garlic yogurt dip) gives Greek flair to a pita meatball wrap. Frozen meatballs fry up in no time in a lightly oiled skillet. Or just nuke them.

DIY gelatin jigglers let you control what goes in them. 4 packets unflavored (unsweetened) gelatin + 4 cups simmering fruit juice + a few hours in the refrigerator = a fun, low-sugar treat. Apple and grape juices are delicious.

HILDON

Gently Sparkling

AN ENGLISH NATURAL MINERAL WATER OF EXCEPTIONAL TASTE

LOW IN SODIUM

FOOT-LONG SUB

Not all chips are potatoes. These days you can get them made from beets, sweet potatoes, pea pods, even hummus!

Need to feed a crowd with packed lunches? Foot-long (or longer) subs are the way to go. Grab a baguette, slice it, stuff it, and cut it.

FRIED EGG VEGGIE SANDWICH

While the skillet is hot, toss in some fresh whole-wheat cheese tortellini, butter, cinnamon, and—just as everything is getting browned and toasty—a bit of brown sugar. Pack it warm or cold.

Don't want a sweet side? Ditch the cinnamon and sugar. Skillet-fry the tortellini with butter and grape tomatoes.

Got leftover veggies? Doesn't matter what type. Pop them onto bread, then top with an extra cheesy egg you fry up at breakfast.

ENGLISH MUFFIN PIZZA, REIMAGINED

The classic English muffin pizza can be reimagined in so many ways. My favorite? Canadian bacon, a slice of tomato, and a bit of cheese. Pop it under the broiler for a couple minutes. Delicious hot or cold.

Got leftover steamed or roasted green beans? Toss them with sesame oil, rice vinegar, sesame seeds, and salt. That's all you need. Also works with leftover broccoli and cauliflower.

LINKED:
SAUSAGES

ROASTED WINTER VEGGIES
WITH CHORIZO

Start to finish: **50 MINUTES (10 MINUTES ACTIVE)**

Servings: **4 MAINS, PLUS LEFTOVERS**

You can substitute any variety of sausage here, but I like the peppery assertiveness of chorizo. Be sure to use fresh chorizo, which should be peeled and crumbled into the pan for cooking. If you use fresh pork sausage, remove the meat from the casings and crumble into the pan. If you use chicken sausage, just slice into thin rounds.

2 pounds fresh chorizo (Mexican chorizo)

1 pound peeled, seeded, and cubed (½-inch cubes) butternut squash

1 pound potatoes, cut into ½-inch cubes

2 large yellow onions, coarsely chopped

4 large carrots, cut into ½-inch chunks

2 tablespoons olive oil

2 tablespoons cornstarch

2 teaspoons ground cumin

2 teaspoons fennel seeds

2 teaspoons kosher salt

1 teaspoon ground black pepper

Heat the oven to 450°F. Line two rimmed baking sheets with foil, then coat well with cooking spray.

Peel the casing away from the chorizo, then break it into large crumbles. In a large bowl, toss the chorizo with the squash, potatoes, onions, and carrots.

Drizzle the oil over the vegetables, then toss. In a small bowl, mix the cornstarch, cumin, fennel, salt, and pepper. Sprinkle over the vegetables, then toss.

Arrange the mixture in an even layer on the prepared baking sheets. Roast for 30 minutes. Increase the oven to broil for another 5 minutes to finish browning.

For a hearty salad, toss leftover roasted veggies with canned white beans, sliced sweet peppers, and a bit of vinaigrette.

Check out the grocer's premade bean salads for easy-to-pack (and healthy!) sides.

ONE DINNER

TWO LUNCHES

Want it hot? Nuke the veggies and sausage, then pop them in a thermos. At lunch, just spoon them onto the prespread bread.

Sesame rice crackers have a rich, soy sauce–like flavor that goes great with sage derby cheese.

A smear of ricotta is the perfect base for leftover roasted veggies and sausage.

VEGGIE, SWEET PEPPER, AND WHITE BEAN SALAD

ROASTED VEGGIE, SAUSAGE, AND RICOTTA SANDWICH

RED BEANS
AND RICE WITH
SAUSAGE

Start to finish: **40 MINUTES**

Servings: **4 MAINS, PLUS LEFTOVERS**

Most recipes for red beans and rice take between 24 and 72 hours. Now that we've all stopped laughing, let's move on to my recipe, which comes together in a fraction of the time.

3½ cups **chicken broth, divided**

1½ cups **long-grain brown rice**

1 **bay leaf**

2 tablespoons **olive oil**

1 large **yellow onion, diced**

1 large **green bell pepper, cored and diced**

1 large **red bell pepper, cored and diced**

4 stalks **celery, chopped**

6 cloves **garlic, minced**

1½ teaspoons **dried thyme**

½ teaspoon **cayenne pepper**

½ teaspoon **smoked paprika**

½ teaspoon **ground cumin**

2 pounds **sweet Italian sausages, cut into chunks**

6-ounce can **tomato paste**

Two 15-ounce cans **red kidney beans, drained**

Kosher salt and ground black pepper

In a medium saucepan over medium-high heat, bring 2½ cups of the broth to a boil. Add the rice and bay leaf, then cover and reduce heat to low. Cook for 35 minutes.

Meanwhile, in a large saucepan over medium-high, heat the olive oil. Add the onion, both bell peppers, the celery, and garlic. Sauté for 10 minutes.

Add the thyme, cayenne, paprika, cumin, and sausage. Cook for another 5 minutes, then add the tomato paste, the remaining 1 cup chicken broth, and beans.

Reduce the heat to simmer and cook until the rice is ready. Once the rice is done, remove the bay leaf and add the rice to the beans. Cook for another 5 minutes, then season with salt and pepper.

Mix leftover red beans and rice (or any thick rice dish), with an egg, then form into patties and sprinkle with breadcrumbs. Fry or bake for high-flavor croquettes. Great hot or cold.

Stir leftover red beans and rice into purchased tomato soup for a hearty, thermos-ready lunch. Accompany with a roll.

365 ORGANIC
EXCELLENT SOURCE OF VITAMIN C

Organic
100% Juice
White

ONE
DINNER

TWO
LUNCHES

Fill frozen mini phyllo dough cups with yogurt and fruit. They'll thaw by lunch for a sweet and healthy treat.

Keep the Cajun theme going by blending fat-free sour cream with Cajun seasoning (check the spice aisle), then use as a veggie dip or toss with broccoli slaw for a side dish with kick.

CROQUETTES

RED BEAN AND RICE
TOMATO SOUP

TOMATO-PEPPER
BRAISED SAUSAGES

Start to finish: **45 MINUTES**
(15 MINUTES ACTIVE)

Servings: **4 MAINS, PLUS LEFTOVERS**

We tend to cook sausages one of just two ways: on the grill or in a skillet. But there are other—and more flavorful—options. This quick braise cooks them in crushed tomatoes, red peppers, and white wine.

2 tablespoons olive oil

2½ pounds sweet or hot Italian pork sausages

½ cup white wine

28-ounce can crushed tomatoes

2 red bell peppers, cored and diced

2 tablespoons capers

2 tablespoons chopped fresh rosemary

3 tablespoons chopped fresh sage

Juice of ½ lemon

¼ cup chopped fresh parsley

Kosher salt and ground black pepper

In a large, deep sauté pan over medium-high, heat the oil. Add the sausages and brown for 4 minutes per side.

Add the wine. It will foam and bubble. Gently shake the pan to loosen the sausages. Add the tomatoes, bell peppers, capers, rosemary, and sage.

Bring to a simmer, reduce the heat to maintain a gentle bubbling, then cover and cook for 15 minutes. Uncover and cook for another 15 minutes.

Remove the pot from the heat and stir in the lemon juice and parsley. Season with salt and pepper.

Serve the sausages with the sauce over rice or noodles, or spooned onto a bun.

Yogurt spiked with cinnamon and honey is a great dessert dip.

Remember, for fun eating, food on a stick always trumps food not on a stick.

Got grains? Got salad. Leftover rice, farro, quinoa, whatever, makes an easy base for an awesome salad. Add finely chopped veggies (whatever you like), some vinaigrette, and you're good to go.

ONE DINNER
TWO LUNCHES

Continue the food-on-stick theme: thread hunks of pur-chased angel food cake (zero fat and reasonable sugar) with fruit.

Pack reheated sausages in a tall thermos for an easy—and hot—sausage roll at lunch.

LUNCH ON A STICK

SAUSAGE ROLL

PROSCIUTTO AND FRESH GOAT CHEESE BAGUETTE

VEGGIE AND SAUSAGE SALAD

Sometimes simple is best. Baguette + fresh goat cheese + prosciutto + a drizzle of honey. That's all.

Pair the kebabs with honey-mustard or mango chutney for dipping.

Kebabs don't need to be hot. And chicken sausage doesn't need to be cooked. Which means this sausage and tomato side comes together in about 1 minute.

Can't be bothered to reheat leftover roasted veggies and sausage? Don't. Add some bread and salad dressing, and call it salad.

Ice cream! Transform frozen fruit into soft serve by pureeing it in the food processor. Bananas, mangos, and peaches are best. Add a pinch of salt and a splash of water. Cinnamon is good, too.

To pack it, pop a thermos in the freezer for 5 or 10 minutes first, then fill it with the ice cream.

LITTLE
BITES

MINI MEATY CHEESY QUICHES

Peaches and cream. Nectarines are great, too!

Find the mini phyllo pastry cups in the freezer section.

Fill each cup with whatever cooked meat (deli is fine) and cheese you have. Whisk 1 egg with salt and pepper, then pour a bit into each. Bake at 400°F for about 10 minutes. Done.

Don't worry about keeping them hot. They are delicious cold.

SANDWICH BITES

For the best roasted cauliflower, cut a head into small pieces, then toss them with olive oil and liberal sprinkles of kosher salt, black pepper, garlic powder, and smoked paprika. Roast on a baking sheet for 20 or so minutes at 400°F.

Doctor roasted cauliflower with canned baked beans and leftover breakfast bacon.

Sandwich bites break big wraps down to size for little eaters. Try a whole-wheat tortilla smeared with peanut butter and sprinkled with cinnamon-sugar.

MEDITERRANEAN-ON-THE-GO

A Mediterranean feast is delicious and easy. Just assemble a plate of your favorite meats, cheeses, and fruits. Done!

If your grocer has a cheese counter that cuts to order, it's an easy way to explore. Ask for small bits of multiple cheeses, then assemble a selection for lunch. When mixing and matching, aim for contrast—try a dry Parmesan or aged Gouda, a tender Manchego or cheddar, and a soft Brie or Camembert.

Don't feel like you have to get fancy. While prosciutto is totally awesome, run-of-the-mill deli ham isn't so bad, either.

Use leftover bacon from breakfast to make a great vinaigrette for your tomatoes—just chop it and add to your favorite purchased or homemade oil-and-vinegar blend.

It's OK to have silly themes . . .

Even healthy lunchers want treats now and then!

PIZZA CUPS

Seasoned toasted pumpkin seeds (often sold as pepitas in the Hispanic and natural foods aisles) are an addictive and filling snack.

Pizza cups! Fill phyllo dough cups with cheese, pepperoni, and cherry tomatoes. Bake until the cheese is lightly browned, then cool and pack.

Most bagels are refined carb bombs. But check the freezer in the natural foods section for sprouted whole-grain bagels. Healthy and delicious.

Top with smoked salmon: a delicious, effortless, and filling source of protein that packs well.

SAMOSAS

Jarred sweet mango chutney from the grocer's international aisle makes the perfect dipping sauce.

Frozen samosas (check the international section of the freezer aisle) heat fast and easy in the morning, and pack even easier in a thermos.

And there are all sorts of treats made from ground almonds, cashews, and coconut.

Indian markets are jammed with awesome lunch items. Chewy treats like these are made from sesame seeds and molasses.

USE YOUR
NOODLE

AMERICAN CHOP SUEY

Start to finish: **30 MINUTES**

Servings: **4 MAINS, PLUS AMPLE LEFTOVERS**

All the built-in vegetables help make this dinner staple a true one-dish meal. And for picky eaters (big and small), all the robust flavors help mask the fact that you're using whole-wheat pasta.

I like pancetta because you can buy it already diced. It also has an amazingly big, bold flavor. But you also could use chopped bacon. Want something lighter? Substitute finely chopped ham steak.

Because pancetta is so rich, I lighten things up on the other end by using lean ground bison instead of the more common ground beef. Ground turkey also would be great.

1 large **yellow onion, chopped**

3 **red bell peppers, cored and diced** (about 3 cups), **divided**

15-ounce can **tomato sauce**

1 tablespoon **soy sauce**

2 teaspoons **Italian seasoning**

3-ounce package diced **pancetta**

3 cloves **garlic, minced**

2 pounds **ground bison**

14½-ounce can **diced tomatoes**

2 cups **beef broth**

12 ounces **whole-wheat elbow macaroni**

Kosher salt and ground black pepper

In a blender, combine the onion, ⅔ of the diced bell peppers, the tomato sauce, soy sauce, and Italian seasoning. Puree until smooth. Set aside.

In a large saucepan over medium-high, brown the pancetta for 3 minutes. Add the garlic and remaining bell pepper and sauté for 3 minutes.

Add the bison and brown, breaking up any large clumps. Add the onion-bell pepper mixture from the blender, the diced tomatoes, broth, and pasta.

Bring to a simmer, then cover and cook, stirring occasionally, until the pasta is tender, 15 to 20 minutes. Season with salt and pepper.

Star fruit's funky shape is a big part of its appeal. But it tastes great, too—a cross between a pineapple and a plum.

Don't be afraid of carb-on-carb. Leftover American chop suey—pasta and all—is crazy delicious on a bun.

Bored by green salads? Who says they have to be green? Try chickpeas, yellow bell peppers, carrots, and tomatoes for a colorful and creative start.

Make it easier to eat more vegetables. Make one large salad on Sunday, then divvy it up over the week.

ONE DINNER

TWO LUNCHES

Apple slices stay fresh thanks to a splash of lemon juice. And they become a "treat" when dipped in a fat-free caramel yogurt.

Lettuce wraps are delicious filled with meaty leftovers such as American chop suey. It also adds a DIY element that kids love.

CHOP SUEY SANDWICH

DIY CHOP SUEY LETTUCE WRAPS

BACON-CAULIFLOWER
MAC AND CHEESE

Start to finish: **30 MINUTES**

Servings: **4 MAINS,
PLUS LEFTOVERS**

The bacon and four cheeses make this mac and cheese seriously indulgent. But the cauliflower and whole-wheat pasta make it virtuous.

For speed, you can skip the breadcrumb and broiling step, making this an easy stovetop meal.

I'm a big believer in have-it-your-way. I like elbow pasta for mac and cheese, but substitute whatever you have. Ditto for my selection of cheeses.

1 pound **whole-wheat elbow pasta**

10 strips **bacon, chopped**

½ medium head **cauliflower, cored and cut into small florets**

2 cups **milk**

1 tablespoon **garlic powder**

½ tablespoon **onion powder**

½ tablespoon **mustard powder**

½ teaspoon **ground black pepper**

¼ teaspoon **cayenne pepper**

4 ounces **cream cheese, cut into chunks**

1½ cups (6 ounces) grated **cheddar cheese**

1½ cups (6 ounces) grated **gruyere cheese**

1 cup grated **Parmesan cheese**

Kosher salt

¾ cup **panko breadcrumbs**

4 tablespoons **butter,** melted

Heat the oven to broil.

Bring a large pot of salted water to a boil. Add the pasta and cook al dente, about 8 minutes. Drain and set aside.

Meanwhile, in a large, deep oven-safe sauté pan over medium heat, cook the bacon for 2 minutes. Add the cauliflower and sauté until lightly browned, about 12 minutes.

Add the drained pasta to the pan and mix well. Add the milk, garlic powder, onion powder, mustard powder, black pepper, and cayenne. Mix well and heat until the milk is hot.

Add the cream cheese, stirring until melted. Sprinkle in the cheddar, Gruyère, and Parmesan, stirring until melted. Season with salt. Leave it in the pan.

In a small bowl, toss the breadcrumbs with the melted butter, then scatter evenly over the pasta. Broil for 2 minutes or until lightly browned.

Sliced apple turns brown when exposed to air. So don't let it be exposed. Slice an apple in half and scoop out the core. Spread a thin (or not!) layer of peanut butter over the cut side, then dunk it in Grape-Nuts, chopped almonds, minced dried fruit, whatever.

It was my son's idea and it totally works.

ONE
DINNER
TWO
LUNCHES

Heat sausage rounds in the same pan as the bacon.

Leftover bacon from breakfast.

Sliced cherry tomatoes add a fresh contrast.

Tortilla chips add a nice crunch.

MAC AND CHEESE GRILLED CHEESE

LEFTOVER MAC AND CHEESE, WITH A TWIST

LEFTOVER PASTA SALAD

Got leftover pasta? You got pasta salad. Toss leftover cold pasta with bottled vinaigrette and whatever veggies you have on hand.

New to dates? They're super sweet, jammed with fiber, and easy to pack. Fill them with cream cheese or wrap them in prosciutto or ham. Or both.

FRIED RAVIOLI

If it's good on top of yogurt or oatmeal, chances are it's good on top of applesauce. Get creative with your toppings.

Fried ravioli? It's easy. Heat some oil or butter in a skillet, add fresh uncooked ravioli, and sauté until browned. Pop in a thermos. This also works with tortellini.

Use the weekend to bake up a batch of whole-wheat banana bread. Whole grains. Produce. All good. My fave recipe? In a food processor, combine 2 bananas, 2 cups white whole-wheat flour, 1½ cups brown sugar, ⅓ cup vegetable oil, 1 egg, 1 teaspoon baking soda, 1 teaspoon cinnamon, ¼ teaspoon ground ginger, ½ teaspoon salt. Process until smooth, transfer to an oiled loaf pan, and bake at 350°F for an hour.

FETTUCCINE
WITH BACON-BASIL PESTO
AND CHICKEN

Start to finish: **30 MINUTES**

Servings: **4 MAINS, PLUS LEFTOVERS (AND AMPLE PESTO)**

The bacon really pushes this pesto over the top. And the recipe makes plenty of extras, so be sure to use it on grilled cheeses, turkey sandwiches, whatever.

1 pound dry **fettuccine pasta**

½ pound **bacon, cooked until crisp**

2½ cups (about 4 ounces) **fresh basil**

¼ cup **pine nuts**

3 cloves **garlic**

1 tablespoon **lemon juice**

½ cup **olive oil**

Kosher salt and **ground black pepper**

3 boneless, skinless **chicken breasts**

2 tablespoons **butter**

14-ounce bag frozen **sliced bell peppers and onions**

1 **lemon, cut into wedges**

Heat the oven to 300°F.

Bring a large saucepan of salted water to a boil. Add the pasta and cook al dente according to package directions. Drain and set aside.

Meanwhile, in a food processor, combine the bacon, basil, pine nuts, garlic, and lemon juice. Process until mostly smooth. With the processor still running, drizzle in the olive oil. Season with salt and pepper, then set aside.

One at a time, cut each chicken breast in half horizontally to create 2 thin cutlets. Season them with salt and pepper.

In a large skillet over medium-high, melt 1 tablespoon of the butter. Add 3 of the cutlets and cook for 2 minutes per side.

Transfer the cutlets to a baking sheet and place in the oven. Repeat with the remaining butter and chicken, placing it in the oven as well.

Return the empty skillet to the heat and add the pepper-onion mixture. Sauté until starting to brown, about 5 minutes. Add the pasta and toss until heated through.

Add the pesto to the pasta, tossing to coat well. Dress the pasta with as much or as little pesto as desired. You will have extra.

Remove the chicken from the oven.

Divide the pasta among serving plates. Top each serving with a chicken cutlet, then squeeze a lemon wedge over each.

Toss fresh strawberries with balsamic vinegar and a pinch each of cinnamon, salt, pepper, and sugar. Awesome spooned over ricotta (cottage cheese or yogurt, too).

The most basic grilled cheese goes from mediocre to magnificent just by adding pesto.

Chicken and pesto really are all you need for a terrific wrap. But jarred sun-dried tomatoes aren't such a bad addition, either.

ONE DINNER

TWO LUNCHES

Worried about a soggy sandwich? The greens should protect the bread, but you also can put the pesto in a container and use it as a dip as you eat.

And since you're already dipping, why not use the pesto to tart up some raw veggies?

PESTO GRILLED CHEESE

CHICKEN AND PESTO WRAP

PASTA
PUTTANESCA

Start to finish: **30 MINUTES**

Servings: **4 MAINS, PLUS EXTRA SAUCE**

Puttanesca is fast and easy to assemble, but tastes like you slaved over it all day. That's because it's built from big, bold flavors, including a whole head of garlic (don't worry, it doesn't taste like a whole head).

While the pasta and sauce (topped with Parmesan, of course) make fine leftovers as is, the sauce is a versatile lunch building block on its own, too.

2 tablespoons **olive oil**

2-ounce can **anchovy fillets,** drained

1 head **garlic,** minced

2 tablespoons **capers,** drained

½ teaspoon **red pepper flakes**

1 large **yellow onion,** diced

2 large **red bell peppers,** cored and diced

1 cup pitted and chopped **kalamata olives**

28-ounce can **crushed tomatoes**

15-ounce can **tomato sauce**

12-ounce box **spaghetti**

Kosher salt and **ground black pepper**

Grated Parmesan cheese, to serve

In a large, deep sauté pan over medium-high heat, combine the olive oil, anchovies, garlic, capers, and red pepper flakes. Sauté, mashing the anchovies with a wooden spoon until they break up and begin to dissolve, about 1 minute.

Add the onion, bell peppers, and olives, then sauté until the vegetables soften and begin to brown, 7 to 8 minutes.

Add the crushed tomatoes and tomato sauce, then bring to a simmer.

Meanwhile, bring a large saucepan of salted water to a boil. Add the spaghetti and cook al dente according to package directions. Drain and divide among serving plates.

Season the sauce with salt and pepper, then spoon over the pasta. Top with grated Parmesan.

Spread a baguette with butter and garlic powder, then wrap in foil and toast. Pop the whole thing (foil and all) into a tall thermos for warm garlic bread.

Heat leftover puttanesca with chicken broth (more or less depending on how thick you want it) and a few tablespoons of peanut butter for a quick and easy soup.

Mix cold leftover puttanesca with purchased tomato soup for an easy chilled gazpacho.

ONE
DINNER

TWO
LUNCHES

Want more substance? Add whatever meat you have handy, or cooked shrimp.

Need a treat that won't tip the scales? Honey sticks won't weigh you down.

Prosciutto-mozzarella rolls are sold alongside the other Italian cheeses. Slice and eat as is, or pop onto bread and broil.

GAZPACHO

AFRICAN PEANUT SOUP

PENNE WITH
SAUSAGE AND BROCCOLINI

Start to finish: **30 MINUTES**

Servings: **4 MAINS, PLUS LEFTOVERS**

This recipe is delicious with any variety of sausage. I like loose sausage meat, but sliced chicken, turkey, or even soy sausage would be great.

And as with all of my pasta dishes, don't get hung up on penne; use any variety. But whatever pasta you use, be sure to follow the directions not to drain it. Using a slotted spoon to transfer it to the skillet brings some of the cooking water with it. This starchy water helps form the sauce.

Broccolini a little too crazy for your kids? Substitute regular broccoli florets, baby spinach (reduce the cooking time), or even peas.

12-ounce box **penne pasta**

2 pounds loose **sausage meat**

1 large **yellow onion**, diced

¼ teaspoon **red pepper flakes**

2 bunches **broccolini** (about 1 pound total), roughly chopped

14-ounce can **artichoke hearts**, drained and halved

1½ cups grated **Parmesan cheese**

Kosher salt and ground black pepper

Bring a large saucepan of salted water to a boil. Add the pasta and cook for 5 minutes. Set the pot aside off the heat. Do not drain.

Meanwhile, heat a large sauté pan over medium-high. Add the sausage, onion, and pepper flakes and brown for 8 minutes or until the meat is nearly cooked.

Add the broccolini and sauté for another 5 minutes. Add the artichoke hearts and sauté for another minute.

Using a slotted spoon, transfer the pasta from the cooking water to the sauté pan. It's OK to get some of the water; this helps form the sauce.

If your pan is not large enough to accommodate everything, you can instead combine everything in a large bowl.

Stir in the Parmesan cheese until melted. Season with salt and pepper.

Making your own soup with leftover pasta is way better than canned. Just add broth, heat, then pop into a thermos.

Head to the bulk aisle and let each family member custom make a snack attack mix.

Add crème fraîche, plain Greek yogurt, mayo, or a splash of vinaigrette to transform leftover pasta with meat and veggies into pasta salad.

ONE DINNER
TWO LUNCHES

Berry jam. Jammed into peanut butter on graham crackers, that is.

Pack applesauce, hot or cold, as you would yogurt—with a selection of toppings.

The sharp flavor of cheddar loves sweet honey and crisp apples.

PASTA SOUP

CREAMY PASTA SALAD

A SALAD TO PUT MEAT ON YOUR BONES

Be fearless with leftovers. Any cooked meat and any cold grain or pasta can be combined for a stick-to-your-ribs salad. Just add a veg or two and you're set.

The cheese doesn't have to go in the salad. Pair hunks of pita bread with chunks of feta cheese and a bit of honey to drizzle over it.

SALADS

CRISPY PASTA SALAD

A fresh take on croutons: sauté leftover cooked pasta with bacon or pancetta until crispy. Let it cool, then toss with your favorite salad fixings.

The best dip— or sandwich spread— ever. Puree 1 avocado + a handful of cilantro + a splash of lime juice + ½ cup of thawed frozen peas (seriously)! Add jalapeños or hot sauce if you like it spicy.

TACO SALAD

It's not a taco shell. It's a stuffed crouton. Fill with whatever salad fixings you've got. Or even stuff it with bacon, lettuce, and tomato for a fresh take on the BLT.

Fresh figs—or dried—are delicious sliced and topped with goat cheese and black pepper.

DIY HOISIN LETTUCE WRAPS

Hoisin sauce (check the Asian aisle) is savory deliciousness in a bottle. Toss it with leftover chicken or steak, lime juice, mint or cilantro, and a splash of hot sauce. Nuke for a minute or so, then pack in a thermos.

Carrots and peanuts (or other nuts) can be snacked on separately or added to the wraps.

Accompany with lettuce leaves for making DIY wraps.

AVOCADO AND SHRIMP PANZANELLA SALAD

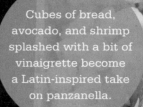

Cubes of bread, avocado, and shrimp splashed with a bit of vinaigrette become a Latin-inspired take on panzanella.

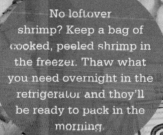

No leftover shrimp? Keep a bag of cooked, peeled shrimp in the freezer. Thaw what you need overnight in the refrigerator and they'll be ready to pack in the morning.

You could pack fruit whole, but slicing it makes it much more appealing. It also lets you dust it with cinnamon and sugar. To prevent browning, toss slices with a bit of lemon or lime juice.

Plantain chips offer a different sort of crunch in your lunch.

SHRIMP AND CHICKPEA SALAD

Craving protein? Cooked shrimp (save yourself the trouble and buy them already cooked and peeled) and canned chickpeas just need parsley, lemon juice, and olive oil. Feta is nice, too.

Stuffed grape leaves are sold alongside the hummus. Or head to an ethnic market and get them in cans for way less (but still good quality).

GREEK MEATBALL AND COUSCOUS SALAD

TEAS'TEA® UNSWEETENED GREEN WHITE TEA AUTHENTICALLY BREWED NATURAL TEA ANTIOXIDANTS

Get your Greek on. Pan-fry frozen meatballs, then toss with purchased tzatziki and spoon over couscous for a cool—and filling— Mediterranean salad.

Raw veggies are way more appealing when paired with something sweet and creamy. Try a blend of low-fat whipped cream cheese and honey mustard.

THE DECONSTRUCTED
DELI

Love a great deli-style sandwich but not sure how to pack the likes of a Reuben or Monte Cristo without them turning to mush by lunch? Got you covered.

The following 12 lunches were inspired by classic sandwiches, all reimagined as hearty salads that are easier to pack and—especially for the little ones—less messy to eat during a rushed lunch.

THE REUBEN

Toss canned or fresh sauerkraut with chopped pastrami for an easy interpretation of this classic sandwich.

Rye croutons (make them or buy them) and thousand island dressing complete the dish.

And don't forget the other deli must-haves.

THE FRENCH DIP

This lunch counter staple becomes a robustly beefy salad. The sandwich version is accompanied by a bowl of warm seasoned beef broth for dipping as you eat. For the salad version, the dip becomes a dressing.

Toss chopped deli roast beef with sliced cucumber and tomato wedges, and pop them over greens.

For the dressing, nuke a bit of beef broth with a bit of olive oil, a spoonful of mustard, and a bit of salt and pepper. Pop it in a small thermos, then drizzle over your salad at lunch.

THE PHILLY CHEESESTEAK

Start with a base of chopped romaine tossed with sliced bread-and-butter pickles, sliced jarred roasted red peppers, and sliced sun-dried tomatoes.

Top with thinly sliced leftover steak and shredded cheese.

Prefer it hot? Toss the sliced steak in a skillet for a couple minutes, then add cheese and pop in a thermos. At lunch, spoon the hot steak and melted cheese over the rest of the salad.

THE MONTE CRISTO

Don't forget the maple syrup. Blend some with oil, vinegar, salt, and pepper for the taste of the classic dip.

Turn the traditional Monte Cristo fillings into a salad—ham, Swiss cheese, cheddar cheese, turkey breast, romaine, and tomato.

Nobody has time in the morning to batter and fry a sandwich for lunch. Instead, top with leftover French toast cut into croutons.

THE BANH MI

This Vietnamese sandwich has become hugely popular, especially in New Orleans. Sliced pork is the traditional choice, but any meat works, so use what you have.

Start by combining romaine with cucumber, cilantro, pickled carrots, and chopped celery. Add whatever meats and cheeses you like.

The dressing should have some bite. Blend mayo with a splash of hot sauce and seasoned rice vinegar.

THE TUNA MELT

Start with a bed of Boston lettuce, then heap on chopped celery, chopped red onion, and Italian-style oil-packed tuna (often called *tonno*, from the Italian).

But the croutons are the best part. Make a grilled cheese sandwich, then cool it and cut it into cubes.

The dressing should be tangy. Try a blend of mayo, mustard, oil, and vinegar.

DRYCK FLÄDER

IKEA FOOD

THE MUFFULETTA

Bring on the taste of New Orleans with a salad version of this classic NOLA grab-and-go.

Start with a base of pickled cauliflower and carrots (check the pickle aisle), then toss on mixed pitted olives, cubes of Swiss, and hunks of pepperoni, salami, and ham.

Don't forget some croutons and a vinaigrette spiked with garlic and oregano.

THE FALAFEL

For the dressing: blend ½ cup plain Greek yogurt, some garlic, ¼ teaspoon ground cumin, ¼ teaspoon ground coriander, a splash of hot sauce, a sprinkle of salt and pepper, and a squirt of lemon juice.

Toss all the classic falafel ingredients in a bowl—chickpeas, diced red onion, diced cucumber, cherry tomatoes, chopped parsley, chopped mint, and some sesame seeds. Drizzle with the dressing.

Or if you've got leftover falafel, just crumble it cold over mixed greens and fresh herbs (parsley, mint, and cilantro are a good start), then add a few tomatoes and some dressing.

THE ELVIS

For the dressing, continue the peanut theme. Blend smooth peanut butter with a splash of cider vinegar and enough water for a smooth consistency, plus salt and pepper.

Start with chopped lettuce, then top it with red onion, carrots, tomato wedges, chopped peanuts, cooked bacon, and crumbled banana chips.

THE BAGEL AND CREAM CHEESE

Start with chopped romaine, then add red onion and thinly sliced cold-smoked salmon. Hunks of fresh goat cheese are more salad-friendly than cream cheese.

For croutons, finely chop an everything bagel, toss with olive oil, and toast in a skillet until just a bit crisp.

THE CALZONE

Make a dressing that tastes like pizza sauce. Blend together a couple sun-dried tomatoes, a bit each of olive oil and balsamic vinegar, and a few pinches of oregano, basil, salt, and pepper.

Top a bed of your favorite greens with a mélange of calzone fillings: chopped red onion, tomatoes, roasted red peppers, black olives, fresh mozzarella, and croutons.

THE BLT

A blend of chopped romaine, iceberg, and arugula keeps the L interesting.

Go for a rainbow of T. And don't forget the intense, savory goodness of sun-dried.

It's not a BLT without mayo. Add a tablespoon to your favorite vinaigrette.

Basic B is good, but not enough. In addition to crumbled bacon, add pancetta "croutons" for B with Bang!

BEEFY

FLANK STEAK WITH
CHIMICHURRI
SAUCE

Start to finish: **30 MINUTES**

Servings: **4 MAINS, PLUS LEFTOVERS**

Think of chimichurri as the pesto of Argentina. It has a tangy, fresh flavor that works great with grilled or roasted meats and vegetables.

Leftover chimichurri is great as a condiment on burgers, grilled cheese sandwiches, or veggie wraps. Also try some blended with sour cream for a dip.

1½ cups packed fresh flat-leaf parsley

¼ cup packed fresh cilantro

1 cup olive oil

⅓ cup red wine vinegar

2 tablespoons dried oregano

1½ tablespoons ground cumin

1½ teaspoons kosher salt, plus extra

3 cloves garlic

¾ teaspoon red pepper flakes

Two 1- to 1¼-pound flank steaks

Ground black pepper

12-inch baguette, thinly sliced

Heat the oven to broil.

In a food processor or blender, combine the parsley, cilantro, oil, vinegar, oregano, cumin, 1½ teaspoons of salt, garlic, and red pepper flakes. Puree until smooth, 2 to 3 minutes. This can be prepared up to a day ahead.

Season the steaks generously with salt and pepper, then arrange them on a rimmed baking sheet. Broil to desired doneness, about 4 minutes per side for medium. Let the steaks rest for 5 minutes.

While the steaks rest, arrange the bread slices on a second baking sheet and toast in the oven for 1 minute or until just barely crisp. To serve, thinly slice the steaks against the grain. Arrange steak strips on toasted baguette slices, then spoon chimichurri over them.

Fry up an extra egg at breakfast and heat up leftover steak right alongside it. Add cheddar or provolone cheese, then turn the whole thing into a sandwich.

Keep sandwiches sog-resistant by toasting them on both sides before packing.

Be sure to include a small spoon for the low- or no-fat sour cream (or plain Greek yogurt).

ONE DINNER
TWO LUNCHES

Drink your fruit! Puree watermelon and a banana for a naturally sweet smoothie.

Thinly sliced leftover steak can be packed hot or cold for a DIY steak fajita kit.

Bocconcini (tiny mozzarella balls) come packed in herby olive oil. Add cherry tomatoes for an instant, flavorful salad.

STEAK, EGG, AND CHEESE SANDWICH

DIY FAJITA KIT

CHILI-GARLIC BEEF
WITH ROASTED BROCCOLI

Start to finish: **25 MINUTES**

Servings: **4 MAINS, PLUS LEFTOVERS**

You'll find chili-garlic sauce in the Asian aisle at the grocer. It gives this dish a medium and totally addictive heat.

If you'd rather steam your broccoli—or add other veggies to the mix—go for it.

Two 12-ounce bags fresh broccoli florets

2 tablespoons olive oil

2 teaspoons garlic powder

1½ teaspoons kosher salt

3 tablespoons butter, divided

1 large yellow onion, thinly sliced

2 pounds flank or skirt steak, thinly sliced against the grain

⅓ cup chili-garlic sauce

6-ounce can tomato paste

Heat the oven to 425°F. Line a rimmed baking sheet with foil, then coat with cooking spray.

In a large bowl, toss the broccoli with the olive oil, then sprinkle with the garlic powder and salt. Toss to coat evenly, then arrange in an even layer on the prepared baking sheet. Roast for 15 minutes, or until tender and browned.

Meanwhile, in a large sauté pan over medium-high heat, melt 2 tablespoons of the butter. Add the onion and cook until just starting to brown, 6 minutes.

Add the steak and cook until just seared, about another 6 minutes.

Stir in the chili-garlic sauce and tomato paste. Toss well, then remove from the heat. Add the remaining 1 tablespoon of butter and toss until melted.

Serve the steak over the roasted broccoli.

Leftover steak also is yummy cold, especially if you top it with fat-free sour cream blended with horseradish.

Don't worry about heating up leftover roasted veggies. Dress them with purchased honey mustard vinaigrette (or make your own) and call it a day.

Got leftover beef stir-fry? Keep it hot in a thermos, then spoon onto a bun at lunch.

ONE DINNER

TWO LUNCHES

Leftover thinly sliced steak makes an awesome soup. Just heat beef broth and add the steak and whatever is handy—in this case, roasted broccoli and frozen corn.

Balsamic vinegar adds Wow! to whatever it touches. Lots of flavor, not a lot of effort. Drizzle it on.

STEAK SOUP

BEEF STIR-FRY SANDWICH

BARBECUE
MARINATED BEEF TIPS
WITH ROASTED CHERRY TOMATOES

Start to finish: **25 MINUTES, PLUS MARINATING**

Servings: **4 MAINS, PLUS LEFTOVERS**

For year-round ease, I wrote this recipe for the broiler. But when weather permits, there's no reason not to toss the beef tips on the grill.

This same recipe works for flank steak or any other quick-cooking cut.

Beef holds up well to marinades, so don't hesitate to pull this together in the morning and let it marinate in the refrigerator all day.

FOR THE STEAK:

1 cup red wine

½ cup packed brown sugar

6-ounce can tomato paste

1 tablespoon lemon juice

1 teaspoon ground cumin

1 teaspoon smoked paprika

1 teaspoon kosher salt

½ teaspoon ground black pepper

3½ pounds steak tips

FOR THE TOMATOES:

2 pints cherry or grape tomatoes

1 tablespoon olive oil

1 tablespoon balsamic vinegar

1 teaspoon kosher salt

½ teaspoon ground black pepper

In a large bowl, whisk together the wine, brown sugar, tomato paste, lemon juice, cumin, paprika, salt, and pepper. Add the steak, turning to coat well. Cover and refrigerate for at least 30 minutes or up to overnight.

When ready to cook, heat the broiler. Line a rimmed baking sheet with foil.

Slice the tomatoes in half, then place them on the prepared baking sheet. Drizzle them with the olive oil, vinegar, salt, and pepper, then toss to coat.

Broil on the center rack for 6 minutes.

Remove the pan from the oven and set a metal cooling rack over it and the tomatoes. Coat the rack with cooking spray.

Remove the steak tips from the marinade and arrange them evenly on the rack over the tomatoes. They will drip some. This is fine.

Return the baking sheet to the oven and broil for 5 minutes, then use tongs to turn the steak. Broil for another 5 minutes, or until desired doneness.

Serve the steaks with the tomatoes and pan juices spooned over them.

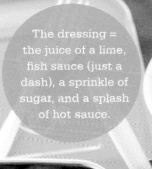

The dressing = the juice of a lime, fish sauce (just a dash), a sprinkle of sugar, and a splash of hot sauce.

Worried your greens will wilt? Pack them in a separate bag, then assemble at lunch.

Toss leftover steak with fresh herbs (cilantro and chives are nice), lime juice, and whatever veggies you like (cherry tomatoes rock) for a salad with big, bold flavors.

ONE DINNER
TWO LUNCHES

Don't forget the garnish. Potent herbs like mint and cilantro pack tons of flavor.

Nuts pack the crunch of croutons, but have protein to fill you up.

Roll slices of fresh goat cheese in chopped dried fruit. They can go on your salad, or on crackers.

No salad greens? No problem. Cukes and carrots are all you need.

THAI-STYLE BEEF SALAD

STEAK SALAD

SLOW COOKER FIVE-SPICE POT ROAST

Start to finish: **8 HOURS ON HIGH**

Servings: **4 MAINS, PLUS LEFTOVERS**

Chinese 5-spice powder is a one-shot powerhouse seasoning for meat. Combined with tomato paste, it turns this simple roast into a savory flavor bomb.

Start this slow cooker roast in the morning as you leave for work. When you get home, the house will smell amazing and dinner will be waiting.

1 tablespoon **olive oil**

2 large **yellow onions,** thickly sliced

4 large **carrots,** cut into 2-inch lengths

5-pound **boneless shoulder chuck roast**

2 tablespoons **cornstarch**

1 tablespoon **5-spice powder**

2 teaspoons **kosher salt**

1 teaspoon **ground black pepper**

1 teaspoon **garlic powder**

6-ounce can **tomato paste**

Drizzle the olive oil over the bottom of a large slow cooker. Arrange the onions and carrots in an even layer. Set the roast on top of the vegetables.

In a small bowl, mix together the cornstarch, 5-spice powder, salt, pepper, and garlic powder. Add the tomato paste and mix to form a thick paste.

Rub the seasoning paste evenly over the roast, working it into the meat; it will be quite thick. Cover and cook for 8 hours on high.

When the roast is done, transfer it to a platter and let it rest for 5 minutes before slicing against the grain.

Use a slotted spoon to transfer the onions and carrots to the platter. Strain the juices in the slow cooker, then serve alongside the roast.

Seasoned baby beets (sold in the refrigerated produce section) add a sweet touch and tons of flavor.

Steak and cheese, please! Heat sliced leftover pot roast, then pop it in a thermos. Pack bread and cheese separately, then assemble at lunch.

Apples aren't the only fruit that can be sauced. Simmer up a compote of plums, peaches, and pears, then accompany with granola. Pack it in a thermos and it's like having warm fruit crisp.

ONE DINNER

TWO LUNCHES

Stuck in the salad doldrums? Move beyond your basic greens. Try arugula or baby kale.

Cold leftover pot roast becomes an easy have-it-your-way roast beef sandwich. Just add mustard and cheese, or what have you.

CHEESESTEAK GRINDER

ROAST BEEF SANDWICH

HOISIN-GLAZED
MEATLOAF

Start to finish: **1 HOUR (15 MINUTES ACTIVE)**

Servings: **5 MAINS, PLUS LEFTOVERS**

Want to cook this faster and make the leftovers easier to pack? Divide the mixture into muffin tins and bake as individual servings, instead of two loaves.

2½ cups **panko breadcrumbs**

2 teaspoons **garlic powder**

1 teaspoon **dried basil**

1 teaspoon **dried oregano**

1 teaspoon **mustard powder**

1 teaspoon **smoked paprika**

1 teaspoons **kosher salt**

2 medium **carrots,** chopped

1 medium **yellow onion,** quartered

1 **egg**

2 pounds **ground beef**

1 pound **loose Italian sausage meat** (mild or hot, to taste)

⅓ cup **hoisin sauce**

⅓ cup **ketchup**

½ teaspoon **hot sauce**

Heat the oven to 375°F. Line a rimmed baking sheet with foil, then coat with cooking spray.

In a large bowl, combine the panko, garlic powder, basil, oregano, mustard powder, paprika, and salt. Set aside.

In a food processor, combine the carrots, onion, and egg. Process until very finely chopped. Add to the breadcrumb mixture and mix well. Add the ground beef and sausage meat, then gently but thoroughly mix. The mixture will be solid and on the dry side.

Divide the mixture in half and transfer one portion to one side of the prepared baking sheet. Form into a loaf about 8 inches long and 2 inches high.

Repeat with the remaining half, forming it into a loaf next to the first, leaving several inches between them.

In a small bowl, mix together the hoisin, ketchup, and hot sauce. Spoon over the top and sides of the meatloaves.

Bake for 40 to 45 minutes, until the meatloaves reach 155°F at the center.

Corn on the cob? Why not? Husk it, nuke it, then stand it up in a thermos.

Pickled vegetables make an easy, tangy side.

If you can do it with burgers, you can do it with leftover meatloaf— sliders!

Crumble warmed leftover meatloaf, then pop it in a thermos. Instant taco meat.

Remember bagel chips? They're back. And they're delicious with cream cheese and strawberries.

ONE DINNER

TWO LUNCHES

MEATLOAF SLIDERS

MEATLOAF TACOS

ROSEMARY-PORT BRAISED BEEF SHORT RIBS

Start to finish: **2 HOURS (20 MINUTES ACTIVE)**

Servings: **4 MAINS, PLUS LEFTOVERS**

Though this recipe braises slowly in the oven for a couple hours, it requires just 20 minutes to prep. This is perfect for a Sunday dinner and sets you up with plenty of lunches for the week.

Remember, when braising meats, reserve some of the cooking liquid. It's great for keeping things moist when reheating and packing.

3 to 3½ pounds boneless beef short ribs

Kosher salt and ground black pepper

2 tablespoons canola or vegetable oil

6-ounce can tomato paste

6 anchovy fillets

2 tablespoons all-purpose flour

1 teaspoon dried thyme

1 teaspoon dried oregano

2 tablespoons chopped fresh rosemary

½ cup tawny port wine

2 cups beef broth

Season the meat on all sides with salt and pepper.

In a large Dutch oven over medium-high, heat the oil until very hot, but not smoking. Add half of the meat and brown for 3 minutes. Transfer to a plate, then repeat with the remaining beef, transferring it to the same plate.

Return the pot to low heat. Add the tomato paste, anchovies, flour, thyme, oregano, rosemary, port, and beef broth. Bring to a simmer.

Return the meat and any juices on the plate to the pot. Return to a simmer, then cover, reduce heat to low, and simmer for 1½ hours or until fork tender.

Use tongs to transfer the meat to a platter. Cover with foil to keep warm. Return the pot to the stovetop over medium-high heat. Boil until thickened and reduced by half, about 2 minutes.

Serve the beef with the sauce ladled over it.

With meat as good as braised short ribs, less can be more. Just heat it with broth or some of the leftover cooking liquid, pop it in a thermos, and pack dinner rolls separately.

Traditional coleslaw too rich for your blood? Buy slaw mix, then dress it with a vinaigrette and chopped dried fruit.

Short ribs—or any leftover beef—are delicious chopped and tossed with cooked pasta and cheese.

Jarred roasted red peppers are a cheap, easy, and versatile veggie. Pat them dry, layer with ham or turkey, then roll up.

ONE DINNER
TWO LUNCHES

Use cheddar if you pack it hot. Use crème fraîche or sour cream if you pack it cold. A splash of hot sauce improves either approach.

DIY BEEF SLIDERS

SHORT RIBS AND PASTA

STEAK NOT-QUITE-TARTARE

Steak tartare? Most of us aren't that brave. But you can come close.

Thinly slice leftover steak that was cooked to medium-rare. Season with vinaigrette and just a touch of Dijon mustard, then pile over chopped romaine.

Keep the semi-raw theme going by topping crisp bread with cream cheese and smoked salmon.

BBQ MEATLOAF

Frozen pretzels will thaw by lunch and offer a fresh take on bread.

Kiwi berries are tiny bombs of sweet strawberry-kiwi flavor. Pop them like grapes—no need to peel.

Don't forget the mustard.

Cook your morning egg, then use the same pan to sear a slab of leftover meatloaf (see recipe on page 158). Drizzled with barbecue sauce, it will stay toasty and moist in a thermos.

VEGETARIAN

ALL-DIP LUNCH

Start with pumpkin hummus: Just puree canned white beans, a bit of canned pumpkin, garlic, a spoonful or so of tahini (sesame paste), salt, lemon juice, and a bit of paprika.

Add veggies and bread or chips and you're good to go.

Then add some packaged conventional hummus, salsa, and spicy peanut sauce to round out your options.

CAPRESE PANZANELLA SALAD

No time to chop fresh fruit? Freeze dried is deliciously crunchy and has no added anything.

Yogurt and applesauce: eat them separately or—even better—stir them together. Or go wild and top with cocoa powder.

Don't toss stale bread. Cube and combine with mozzarella, cherry tomatoes, and basil for easy panzanella salad. Pack olive oil and balsamic on the side.

DOCTORED HUMMUS

Hummus practically begs to be doctored. Top it with what you like and it changes from a side to a main. I like hard-boiled egg, chopped scallions, and red onions.

A veg dip to move you way beyond your ranch rut: strawberry jam, a splash of balsamic vinegar, a splash of olive oil, and a bit of salt and pepper.

PUFF PASTRY WITH GOAT CHEESE AND ROASTED RED PEPPERS

Vegan jerky? It's no oxymo-ron. It's a tasty, healthy snack.

Don't dress salads until you're ready to eat. The acid wilts the greens.

Best vinaigrette ever: 3:1 ratio of oil and vinegar, a pinch of kosher salt, a grind of pepper, and a heaping spoonful of strawberry or other fruit jam.

Frozen puff pastry goes from fridge to finish in minutes. Bake off squares in the toaster oven, then top with goat cheese and slices of jarred roasted red peppers.

5-MINUTE POLENTA

Tubes of prepared polenta (check the Italian aisle) go from cylinder to sensational in minutes. Cut off the amount you want, then heat in a saucepan with milk or broth. Mash it and you're done.

Pair the warm polenta with left-over or purchased pasta sauce in a thermos.

Tired of the same old hummus? Pick up prepared artichoke spread and pair with breadsticks for some-thing different.

Don't forget the Parmesan.

COLD PEANUT NOODLES

Leftover spaghetti gets new life as cold peanut noodles. Mix peanut butter, soy sauce, hot sauce, and garlic powder, then toss. Or just use bottled peanut sauce.

Mandarin orange segments can be snacked on solo or dunked in fat-free chocolate yogurt.

VEGGIE PANZANELLA SALAD

Veggies + bread + vinaigrette = endless varieties of panzanella.

Save yourself the trouble of cooking corn. It's best cut straight off the cob and eaten raw. Not in season? Drain and dump from the can.

Pack a treat without packing guilt. The grocer's natural foods aisle has (slightly) more virtuous versions of classic treats—this one is made with brown rice and brown rice syrup.

SOUPS
& SUCH

SPEEDY
SWEET HEAT
CHILI

Start to finish: **30 MINUTES**

Servings: **4 MAINS, PLUS LEFTOVERS**

1 tablespoon **smoked paprika**

2 teaspoons **chili powder**

2 teaspoons **ground cumin**

2 teaspoons **dried oregano**

2 teaspoons **garlic powder**

1 teaspoon **cinnamon**

1 teaspoon
mustard powder

4 strips **bacon, finely chopped**

2 tablespoons **olive oil**

2 pounds **sirloin tips,
finely chopped**

2 pounds 90 percent
lean **ground beef**

1 large **yellow onion,** diced

1 large **apple,** peeled,
cored, and diced

6-ounce can **tomato paste**

15-ounce can **tomato sauce**

¼ cup minced **Peppadew peppers**

2 tablespoons minced
pickled jalapeños

2 tablespoons **cider vinegar**

**Kosher salt and ground black
pepper**

The blend of sirloin and ground beef is part of what gives this chili such an amazing texture. The easiest way to chop the sirloin is to pop it in the processor for a few seconds. But if you do it by hand, don't sweat the size. Larger chunks are fine, too.

If you can't find Peppadew peppers (a sweet, brined tiny red pepper), substitute roasted red peppers.

In a large stockpot over medium-high heat, combine the paprika, chili powder, cumin, oregano, garlic powder, cinnamon, and mustard powder. Toast the seasonings, stirring constantly, for 30 seconds.

Add the bacon and olive oil, then sauté for 2 minutes.

Add the chopped sirloin tips and ground beef and cook for 8 minutes, breaking up any large clumps.

Add the onion, apple, tomato paste, tomato sauce, Peppadews, jalapeños, and vinegar, then bring to a simmer. Cook for 10 minutes, then season with salt and pepper.

Warmed and packed in a thermos, leftover chili just needs cheese and a bun.

Blue cheese dip makes any veggie way more appealing. Buy it or make it by mixing a little crumbled blue cheese in ½ cup of low-fat sour cream. Spike it with a splash of hot sauce.

No phyllo cups? Coat a mini muffin tin with cooking spray, then spoon the chili-egg mixture right in and bake.

Mix leftover chili and an egg, then spoon into frozen phyllo pastry cups and bake for 10 minutes at 400°F.

ONE DINNER
TWO LUNCHES

Don't do blue cheese? Hummus, baba ghanoush, roasted red pepper dip, and pesto are great alternatives that won't trigger "No more ranch dressing!" grumbles.

Got leftover French toast? Skewer it for dunking in a container of maple syrup. Also works for pancakes and waffles.

CHILI SANDWICH

CHILI CUPS

MEATBALL AND VEGGIE SOUP

Fruit-in-a-cup? It can be a better choice than you'd think. Plenty of brands now offer no-added-sugar varieties.

It's also an easy way to pack fruits you wouldn't normally consider lunch box–friendly, like grapefruit.

Simmer frozen meatballs and a what-have-you of leftover veggies in purchased broth while you eat breakfast. By the time you're done eating, you've got a thermos-worthy soup.

TOMATO SOUP WITH GRILLED CHEESE CROUTONS

Frying an egg for breakfast? When you're done, use the pan to make a grilled cheese, then cut it up for awesome croutons to add to a thermos of tomato soup.

Hollow out half a small papaya (don't eat the black seeds inside it), then fill with mixed berries for a fruit salad with an edible bowl.

SPEEDY
BEEF STEW

Start to finish: **45 MINUTES (15 MINUTES ACTIVE)**

Servings: **4 MAINS, PLUS LEFTOVERS**

Beef stews typically take hours to make. My version avoids the time suck by using sirloin tips instead of more traditional stew meat (which takes way longer to get tender). No cider handy? Substitute beer or another cup of beef broth.

2 tablespoons olive oil

3 pounds sirloin beef tips,
cut into 1-inch chunks

4 large carrots,
cut into 1-inch chunks

1 pound new potatoes,
quartered

1 large yellow onion, diced

3 cloves garlic, minced

28-ounce can
crushed tomatoes

1 cup apple cider

1 cup beef broth

1 tablespoon
chopped fresh rosemary

1½ teaspoons smoked paprika

1 teaspoon dried thyme

1 teaspoon mustard powder

Kosher salt and
ground black pepper

In a large pot over medium-high, heat the oil. Add the beef in batches to avoid crowding the pan, and sear just lightly, about 2 minutes; it should still be rare.

Use a slotted spoon to transfer the beef to a plate.

Return the pot to the heat and add the carrots and potatoes. If the pan is too dry to easily sauté the vegetables, add a splash of olive oil.

Sauté until the potatoes begin to brown, about 5 minutes. Add the onion and garlic, then continue to cook until the onion is tender, about another 5 minutes.

Add the tomatoes, cider, broth, rosemary, paprika, thyme, and mustard powder. Bring to a simmer, cover, and cook until the potatoes are tender, about 15 minutes.

Return the beef to the pot, as well as any juices that have accumulated on the plate. Simmer for 5 minutes, then season with salt and pepper.

Apples + gelatin = fun snack. Use a melon baller to hollow out half an apple. Brush it with lemon juice, then fill it with gelatin dessert and refrigerate until set.

Don't overthink side salads. Cucumbers, feta, and scallions are all it takes to get you eating your veggies.

ONE
DINNER

TWO
LUNCHES

Just spoon leftover stew into empanada shells, fold, crimp, and bake until lightly browned. Delicious warm or not. You'll find empanada shells in the freezer section with the Hispanic foods.

Pack reheated stew in a thermos, then just spoon it onto a roll and top with cheese come lunchtime.

BEEF AND VEGETABLE EMPANADAS

STEW GRINDER

COLD CHOWDER

Cold chowder? Yup. And it's insanely good. Season a can of unsweetened coconut milk with ½ teaspoon curry powder, then add cooked peeled shrimp and canned corn kernels. Salt, pepper, a squeeze of lemon juice, maybe some hot sauce, and you're done.

RICOTTA: the ultimate salad starter. Just add jarred marinated artichokes, some arugula, and whatever else gets you going.

DIY BAKED BEANS

Nuke some purchased corn-bread and keep it warm in a spare thermos to enjoy with the beans.

There is nothing wrong with canned baked beans. They are healthy, filling, and stay toasty in a thermos for hours. Treat them like a baked potato—top them with what you like: sour cream, cheese, scallions, bacon, whatever.

CASHEW CURRY
CHICKEN
WITH SQUASH

Start to finish: **35 MINUTES**

Servings: **4 MAINS, PLUS LEFTOVERS**

This is a simple, speedy, but delicious chicken curry. Add and adapt as you see fit. If cashews aren't your style, substitute pistachios or just leave them out.

For weeknight ease, I call for curry powder. The flavor isn't as complex as blending your own seasonings . . . but life is complex enough. At least dinner should be easy.

1 head **cauliflower,** cut into small florets

4 tablespoons **olive oil**

1½-pound **butternut squash,** peeled, seeded and cut into ½-inch chunks (about 1 pound cubed flesh)

1 large **yellow onion,** diced

4 cloves **garlic,** minced

2 pounds boneless, skinless **chicken thighs,** cut into 1-inch chunks

1½ tablespoons **curry powder**

1 cup **whole cashews**

1 cup **coconut milk**

½ cup **golden raisins**

Kosher salt and **ground black pepper**

1 tablespoon **lime juice**

2 tablespoons chopped fresh **cilantro**

Place the cauliflower florets in a large saucepan with about 1 inch of water. Bring to a boil, then cover and simmer for 7 minutes or until just tender. Drain and set aside.

Meanwhile, in a large skillet over medium-high, heat 2 tablespoons of the oil. Add the squash and sauté until lightly browned, about 10 minutes.

Add the onion and garlic, then sauté 3 minutes. Transfer the mixture to a plate and set aside.

Return the skillet to the heat and add the remaining oil. Add the chicken and brown on all sides, about 5 minutes total.

Sprinkle the curry powder and cashews over the chicken, then sauté for another minute. Return the vegetables to the skillet and toss well.

Add the coconut milk and raisins, stir gently, and bring to a simmer. Season with salt and pepper, then stir in the lime juice and cilantro.

Serve the chicken over the cauliflower.

Whether you make it or buy it, a mango lassi (think Indian smoothie) is a great choice with curry. To make, blend 1 cup frozen mango, 1 cup milk or plain yogurt, and a pinch of cardamom or cinnamon, then pour into a thermos.

Chicken curry, or any curry, is a great way to doctor up purchased soup. Grab a container of creamy potato soup, add leftover curry, heat it, and pack it.

Leftover curry needs nothing more than a thermos to stay warm and some creative serving options.

ONE DINNER
TWO LUNCHES

Purchased naan (Indian flat bread) is an obvious choice. But scoop-shaped corn tortilla chips—while perhaps not traditional—are fun and delicious.

Turn watermelon into a treat with just a bit of honey for dipping.

CHIPS AND LEFTOVER CURRY DIP

CURRIED SOUP

My son and I have a tradition. The night before his last day of school, I bring him to a bakery. He's allowed to fill his lunch box with whatever he likes.

It comes just once a year, so go a little crazy.

ACKNOWLEDGMENTS

Writing a cookbook is an amazing alchemy that extracts scribbles and rants from a caffeinated ether and transforms them into something real enough to spill coffee on. It is grueling, breathtaking, and almost never solitary. I have many to thank.

Rachael Ray, for paving the way in so many ways. And for seeing the promise in this crazy peek into the lunch box inside my head. She got it. Instantly. And for that—and her unwavering support—I am immensely grateful.

Kathleen Carroll, Lou Ferrara, Nekesa Moody, and Lisa Tolin, my bosses at The Associated Press. They have entrusted me with the best gig in the food world and given me the freedom to make it even better. Thank you.

Charlie Dougiello . . . Friend? Publicist? Go-between? Collaborator? Co-conspirator? It doesn't really matter. Thank you. Seriously.

Johanna Castillo and Lisa Sciambra, and the Atria Books team who pulled this all together. Thank you for working so hard to make my ideas come to life.

Eric Lupfer, my agent at William Morris Endeavor, for continuing to be the voice of reason in my increasingly cluttered head.

Matthew Mead, food photographer, stylist, and fellow publishing junkie, for once again transforming my drivel into something beautiful.

Alison Ladman and the rest of my AP pit crew. You are essential. And you may never, ever leave. That is all. Thank you.

The readers of my blog, LunchBoxBlues.com. Knowing the world is watching—and is so wonderfully supportive—makes it easier to be creative while serving time in the lunch box trenches.

Holly Ramer, my wife, for her support, patience, and willingness to take a backseat to the contents of our son's lunch box. Love you.

And Parker, the munchkin who started it all. The lesson, of course, is that no matter how much we plan and prepare, often the best things in life are the unexpected, the things we have not planned and prepared for. Work hard, read hard, and be open to anything. The rest will take care of itself. I love you.

AUTHOR'S NOTE:
THE INSPIRATION

He was bound to ask eventually.

"Daddy, why do you take pictures of my lunch every morning?"

Fair question. But how do you explain to a kid raised without TV or the Internet that Daddy writes a blog about his lunch? And that every day he shares that seemingly private meal with thousands of vicarious eaters online.

Until that moment, I'd decided you don't explain.

It started as a suggestion from a friend. We were comparing lunch packing strategies, and I rattled off Parker's favorites. It was the Star Wars–inspired egg sandwich I'd dubbed the "Obi Wan-wich" that pushed her over the edge.

"You have got to start a blog about this stuff," she urged.

I can be dense at times, so it was a while before I took her seriously. Eventually I did, and it's been a crazy ride since. Even as I did media interviews and appearances—including going on Martha Stewart's show to teach her how to make Parker's favorite pulled pork sandwich—I kept my son mostly in the dark.

For some reason I decided that no matter how public his lunches had become, he still should consider them a private exchange between the two of us.

Because lunch has a powerful pull on the emotions of childhood. As adults, we linger over and get all lyrical about the powers of wonderful dinners. We talk about them, plan them, labor over them.

But for children, lunch wields this power.

Lunch is when children are entrusted to eat outside the purview of parents. It's an eat-with-your-friends, not a get-grilled-by-Mom-and-Dad-about-your-day. And for children who brown bag it, it is as concrete a tether to the love of home as they are likely to encounter as they trudge through their long days.

Not that every lunch I pack for my kid ends up some Rockwellian moment.

Parker came home disappointed with his lunch one day—leftover kangaroo steak and elk sausage. The problem was the other kids at the table. Apparently the food—which he'd devoured—didn't get the reaction Parker had been hoping for.

"My friends didn't say anything when I told them I had kangaroo and elk," he muttered.

I considered telling him his friends may not have believed him. Or that since he brings unusual foods fairly often, maybe they just weren't surprised. Then I thought better of it. Lunch packing is stressful enough. I'm not willing to add impressing a gaggle of grade-school boys to the criteria.

When I was his age, I was more concerned with the militant nuns who patrolled my school's lunchroom than with what my friends thought. My 9-going-on-19-year-old has no idea how easy he has it. My angst over the occasional unfinished vegetable in his lunch is a pleasantry compared to the fury such a sin unfurled when Sister "Tomato Face" Theresa was on duty.

Lunches were eaten. Lunch boxes were inspected to ensure it. It was that simple.

Every day Mom packed me the same cheddar cheese and mustard on whole wheat. Every day she dutifully trimmed off the crusts that made me gag.

Until the day she forgot.

Of course I didn't eat the crusts. Of course I left those ribs of mustardy wet bread in my clangy metal *Empire Strikes Back* lunch box. And of course Sister Theresa found them.

"We do NOT waste food, Mr. Hirsch!" she growled, her cheeks and nose taking on their namesake blush.

I sobbed and wailed and begged. Until inspiration hit.

"I'll make my mother eat them!" I blurted.

Somehow, the blush receded. Somehow it worked. I'd thrown my mother to the nuns, but I didn't have to eat those soggy, gaggy crusts.

Thirty years later, my son bursts each day from his classroom. And he knows that too much but-I-didn't-have-time-to-eat-my-carrots will get him an eye roll. And that it will not be me eating the carrots—or the crusts—when we get home.

So when did I tell Parker about the blog? The tipping point came about a year ago, when Rachael Ray offered to turn my blog into this book. It seemed like a good time to finally give him a seat at the table.

His reaction?

"Oh I know," he said calmly. "A friend at school reads it with his mom every day and he tells me about it all the time."

INDEX

ABOUT THE AUTHOR

J. M. Hirsch is the national food editor for The Associated Press. He blogs about the trials, tribulations, and triumphs of his son's lunches at LunchBox Blues.com and tweets as @JM_Hirsch. His previous books include *High Flavor, Low Labor: Reinventing Weeknight Cooking* and *Venturesome Vegan Cooking.* He lives in New Hampshire with his son, wife, and too many cats.

© SHARON RAMER

ABOUT THE PHOTOGRAPHER

Matthew Mead is the food photographer for The Associated Press. He also is a regular contributor to *Better Homes and Gardens* magazine and the former style editor of *Country Home* magazine. He has written and photographed numerous books and produces his own magazine. His work has appeared in ad campaigns for Lowes, Target, Pottery Barn, Dove Chocolate, and Stonewall Kitchen. He blogs at HolidayWithMatthewMead.com.

© MATTHEW MEAD